Adventures of a Lifetime
TRAVEL TALES FROM AROUND THE WORLD

Edited by Janna Graber

WORLD TRAVELER PRESS
COLORADO, USA

Copyright © 2014 by World Traveler Press
Introduction copyright © 2014 by Janna Graber

All rights reserved. No part of this publication may be reproduced, distributed or transmitted in any form or by any means, without prior written permission.

World Traveler Press
Colorado USA
www.WorldTravelerPress.com

Cover design by Julius Broqueza

Adventures of a Lifetime: Travel Tales from Around the World
First edition

ISBN 978-0-9908786-2-9 (Print)
ISBN 978-0-9908786-3-6 (E-book)

"The purpose of life is to live it, to taste experience to the utmost, to reach out eagerly and without fear for newer and richer experience."

— Eleanor Roosevelt

CONTENTS

Introduction 7

Safari on Ice – *Manitoba, Canada*
Peter Mandel 15

Deserted in the Gobi – *China*
Richard McCulloch 25

In Ruins – *Peru*
Claire Ibarra 39

The Naked Truth – *New Guinea*
Bruce Northam 51

Filling in the Holes – *Latvia*
Janna Graber...61

Monkey Wrench – *Indonesia*
Asia Nichols 77

Letters from the Countryside – *Czech Republic*
Todd Pitock 89

Hiking the Ancient Nakasendo Way – *Japan*
Peter Mandel 105

Feeling Tanzania – *Tanzania*
Kimberley Lovato 113

Stepping Up to the Challenge – *Iceland*
Mim Swartz...125

Girding the Globe – *Around the World*
Dan Leeth 133

Paradise Lost – *Hawaii, USA*
Gina Kremer..149

Lionfish Quest – *Belize*
Darrin DuFord 163

Healing Heights of Machu Picchu – *Peru*
Erin Byrne.. 179

Fear in Srinagar – *Kashmir*
Mariusz Stankiewicz... 189

Walks on the Wild Side – *Uganda*
Peter Mandel 205

Last Trip to Venice *Italy*
Mim Swartz 215

The Day the Earth Moved – *Japan*
Aaron Paulson.. 225

Sailing Down Under – *Australia*
Maggie Cooper 239

Of Nomads and Whales – *Mali*
James Michael Dorsey 249

Pilgrimage to Mount Kailash – *Tibet*
Nayanna Chakrbarty 257

Honeymoon for Three – *Alaska, USA*
Michael Engelhard... 269

Dream at the End of the World – *Antarctica*
Robert N. Jenkins... 283

Farewell Tour – *Turkey*
David Richard Teece 291

JANNA GRABER

INTRODUCTION

You can tell a lot about a person by the images on their phone or computer screen. My screen usually rotates a series of photos from places I've visited and loved — tiny Swiss villages, remote Asian rainforests and some of my favorite world-class cities.

But lately, I've focused on a photo from Arnhem Land, a rugged Aboriginal homeland in the far reaches of Australia's Northern Territory. Reachable only by bush plane, Arnhem Land is a remote part of the world that few ever visit.

The night I took that photo, I was on a bush safari in the Outback. We had spent the day following Max Davidson, the rugged outdoorsman leading our adventure, on a trek through the Australian bush. He had shown us caves filled with 5,000-year-old Aboriginal art, and "bush tucker" that we could pick and eat along the way.

I was sunburned and covered in insect bites, but I couldn't have been happier.

When the sun started to sink lower on the horizon, Max suggested we take his small pontoon boat onto the billabong for sunset. As we floated slowly on the water, I watched thousands of birds soar overhead, their images small silhouettes against the pink and yellow skies. Crocs eyed us as we skimmed past, and a tiny "Jesus" bird skipped across the flowering lily pads for destinations unknown.

Just when I thought it couldn't get any better, Max pulled out a bottle of wine and a plate of cheese. We stopped the boat and enjoyed our fare as the sun dipped below the horizon. At that moment, I pulled out my camera and snapped one precious image.

It was a moment that I knew I would remember for decades — an adventure of a lifetime.

The world is full of special places like this — and rich with adventures. In this unique collection of travel stories, 21 writers from around the globe share some of their most incredible adventure travel experiences.

Adventure can mean different things to different people. For Nayanna Chakrbarty, it meant a challenging pilgrimage to Mount Kailish in Tibet, while Peter Mandel chose to hike the ancient Nakasendo Way in Japan. Todd Pitock set out on his bike to discover a different side of the Czech Republic, and Michael Engelhard took his brother and sister-in-law on an unusual Alaskan honeymoon.

Sometimes, adventure travel means confronting our fears, such as when Erin Byrne faced her dread of heights during an unforgettable trip to Machu Picchu and Mim Swartz stepped out of her comfort zone while snowmobiling with strangers in Iceland. Maggie Cooper's determination helped her learn how to sail so she and her partner could cross one of Australia's most dangerous straits, while Claire Ibarra changed her mindset to make the best of a difficult situation in Peru.

Adventure travel can take unexpected turns. Gina Kremer set out for a relaxing Hawaiian hike only to find her life in danger when she lost her way, and Bruce Northam never expected to find himself playing Frisbee – naked – with a tribe in New Guinea.

When travel leads you into tenuous situations you can't control, adventure can take a frightening turn, such as when Richard McCulloch and his friend were unceremoniously dumped in the Gobi Desert or Mariusz Stankiewicz found himself in the middle of conflict in Kashmir.

Aaron Paulson's quiet life as a teacher in Japan took an unexpected turn during a destructive earthquake, while Darrin DuFord found unexpected adventures below the seas near Belize.

This collection also includes some hilarious travel experiences, such as Dan Leeth's unconventional cruise around the world or Asia Nichols' unsettling encounter with monkeys in an Indonesian forest. And Robert Jenkins learned a few new things about penguins on his dream trip to Antarctica.

Sometimes adventure means stepping outside of your own culture and into another, such as James Michael Dorsey's camel trek with the "Blue Men" of Mali or my own journey to Latvia, in search of roots that had been tragically lost. Kimberley Lovato tells of getting to know Tanzania in a new way, while David Richard Teece takes one last tour of Turkey.

These are just some of the stories in Adventures of a Lifetime. Whatever your definition of adventure travel, I hope you enjoy this entertaining collection of stories. Most of all, I hope they inspire you to create adventures of your own.

Janna Graber is an American travel journalist, editor and producer who has covered travel in more than 38 countries. She fell in love with exploring other countries and cultures while studying abroad in Austria, and has been hooked ever since. She is the managing editor at GoWorldTravel.com, and has written for Parade, Reader's Digest, Outside, The Chicago Tribune and many more. Read more of her work at jannagraber.com or follow her on Twitter @AColoradoGirl.

*Adventures of
a Lifetime*
TRAVEL TALES FROM
AROUND THE WORLD

PETER MANDEL

SAFARI ON ICE
Manitoba, Canada

Polar bears are everywhere these days. Peering at you from cans of Coke, eating ice cream in ads and padding around in cartoons with penguins (who belong at the other pole).

Polar bears are everywhere. Everywhere, that is, but where they should be: on ice floes in the far, far north.

The world's largest land carnivores are in trouble. Since they live and hunt part time on frozen chunks of ocean, declines in sea ice could cut back their numbers by two-thirds by 2050. Or worse. They could become extinct.

To me this shot up a flare of alarm. I wanted to write checks to charities who would try to help them. I wanted to buy bear books. I wanted to spend hours at the zoo.

The more I read and watched, the more I realized: It didn't work.

I needed to see these big white guys in the wild before it was too late.

*****

It is October, late in the month, and I sign up for a tour to the not-quite-North Pole. It is a safari, a weird one, run by Natural Habitat Adventures. Instead of lions or elephants or leopards, we will be aiming for bear. Polar bears, that is — those that are roaming the sub-arctic tundra near an outpost called Churchill, Manitoba.

When I look at a map, I note that the Arctic Circle is at latitude 66.6. Churchill, on the edge of Hudson Bay, sits at 60. I buy myself a hat with ear flaps. In a basement box I turn up a pair of boot socks — the kind that are as thick as mittens, the kind that take up all the room in your shoes.

In Winnipeg, it is snowing already. We cram into a chartered prop plane that says on its side that it is run by "Calm Air." As advertised, the atmosphere under our wings is tepid for about an hour. Then there are bumps. And, slightly farther north, some drops.

Soon we are ski-jumping at thousands of feet up. After a dip, I make a grab for my cup of juice. I've got it, but the liquid inside goes wild. It leaps up on its own then collapses in my lap.

I try to distract myself with the in-flight magazine. "Winter Living," teases the cover. "Cure your cabin fever. Cook up comfort food. Check out our cool cold-weather clothes!"

I decide it's going to be a very long ride.

Churchill, I discover, is a scattering of streets and insulated sheds, but it is right where polar bears arrive each fall in late October and early November to wait for Hudson Bay to freeze. As soon as it does they pad out onto the ice for winter hunting of seals.

Tundra, tundra everywhere. Our guide up here, a German named Matthias, tells us that "tundra" is the land that doesn't have any trees, and that the patches with scraggly forest are called "taiga."

Did someone say forest? You can spot a few toothbrush-thin spruce trying to grow. But mostly there is wind and snow and a kind of distant cousin of daylight. I check my watch: 1:43 pm. This can't be right.

Instead of a sun, someone has screwed a Soft White bulb into the sky. And they've stuck it in just over the horizon. According to this, it should not be earlier than 5.

On the ride from the airport, we tourists shout and point. Three shapes that look like pictures in calendars plod along right by the side of the road. We are amazed. It is a mother bear and cubs. Lens caps are dropped, windows on the bus are ajar, and shutters snap and snap.

These are not zoo bears. Not at all. Their fur is puffy, not yellowish or matted. And while the cubs are shy, their mom is confident in a way that's not easy to describe. She leads the pack, she scans, but she's not wary like other animals I have watched in the wild.

The cubs are toddler princes. She is the white queen.

We are in her world now, and it is we who unload our bags into a kind of cage. Our home for five days will be a specially-built movable tundra lodge: four train-style cars linked together and jacked up on fat ATV wheels. We're high enough for safety, but it feels like any cub could hop up onto our decks.

Our sleeping car is toasty, thanks to an industrial-strength iron stove set up in an alcove that is whistling while it throws us heat. Each of us gets a private compartment that's about the size of first-class berths on Amtrak: There's an upper and lower bunk, a window and some hooks and cubbies to stow your gear.

First things first. I strip off my boot socks and drape them near the stove. I do the same with my hat.

"My ears are ice," complains Roberta Bakos, who tells us she lives in the south. "Miami," she says. "Miami Beach!"

I should be sympathetic, but I'm not. My toes have been dead since Winnipeg. Now they are itching from the warmth and from the wool of the socks.

I rub and stamp. Jump and scratch. I refuse to move from the stove.

In addition to our Pullman bunkroom, the tundra train has cars for lounging and dining. It has between-car decks with railings and steel mesh gratings. And it has bears.

Bears licking the tires under the lodge. Bears snuffling inches from our shoes out on deck. Bears growling and arguing. And bears staring up the open drains when you are trying to get clean.

When I take a shower, I look down while pouring shampoo and see a medium-sized male watching carefully from below. I am embarrassed. But the bear is not.

I rinse off some soap. He rears up closer to the drain. I run the water hot. He shows me his nose and teeth. I crank the knob for pressure, pull it down as hard as it will go. His tongue comes out, just slightly. It flaps. He smacks it. He is having a drink.

Time to towel off.

Our welcome dinner is a type of seafood stew. It's just the thing for the cold, and I find I'm craving beer and chunks of butter and bread. Someone notices that a pot of something is steaming out on deck. One of the cooks is stirring, stirring.

"Is it dessert?" asks Bakos.

It is not. It is a broth with leftover scales and fishbones and shells. "We keep it bubbling for the bears," explains Matthias. "Of course they like this smell."

After coffee we get a Matthias briefing. "Well, you see some bears already on the way. You see them outside and under the decks. But do you know what you are seeing?"

We think we do. But we are wrong.

"The male," says Matthias, "he can weigh two times as much as the Siberian tiger." I remember the one in my shower. "Of all the species of bear," he adds, "he is most likely to prey on humans." I think of my shower bear again.

According to Matthias' chart, a grown-up male can tip the scales at 800 pounds, 1,000 pounds, even 1,500. Is this a mistake? He points to the chart. "The polar bear," he says, "is big. It is sometimes 9, sometimes 9 ½-feet long."

When other facts like this pop out, people start scribbling notes.

*Female polar bears are only about half the size of males. But, when they're pregnant, they get fat, doubling their weight.

*A polar bear's skin isn't white, it's black. (This causes frowns.)

*If you try to take an infrared shot of a polar bear, good luck. They're so well insulated, they're invisible in infrared — except for their breath.

*And, yes, polar bears are in trouble. They swim from ice floe to ice floe. And with so much ice melting off, they've had to swim farther — often struggling, sometimes drowning — in their push to find food.

Our bears are still on land where they are safe and where we can meet them. Every night they cluster around to smell our stew. To stare in our showers. And to have their squabbles — private disagreements — in the dark.

When it gets late we stop looking down for a little while and look up. At Northern Lights aglow — in-the-dark Frankenstein green.

Every day, we pile into a sort of moon-buggy to ride away from the lodge in search of yet more bears. The buggy is cold, and we get bitten by an arctic wind that whistles with the zest of the disturbed.

Someone shouts about a snowy owl they can see. Maybe it's a rock, I say. It is probably an owl, decides our guide. When it swivels its feathery head we know for sure.

Seconds later we spot an arctic fox that pops up and disappears behind a bank of snow. He is whiter than the white of the landscape, and surprisingly small. My cat, Sam, outweighs him by a good 5 pounds, but this fox is fast — trotting and darting until he is gone.

Our last day of the tour is spent in town and we are warned that there can be bears in Churchill, too.

"It isn't good," says a local guide we meet here, "but before we closed it, they would come to have some dinner at the dump."

"Bears are aggressive," adds Matthias, "and they are sometimes creative. They eat plastic, Styrofoam, entire bags of garbage — that's including the bag. Anything people throw away."

The last time anyone got mauled here was in 1983, we are told. For reasons no one can explain, a local man went for a walk at night with jacket pockets filled with meat. A polar bear ate him and the pocketed meat as a single meal.

None of this is reassuring, and we look carefully around corners and spend a lot of our time inside bars and stores. "At least," says Roberta Bakos, who is buying a statue of an arctic walrus, "it means there are still enough of the bears for us to have to worry."

"Still enough," agrees Matthias. "To do what polar bears do."

I'm glad to hear it. But when I go to the edge of Churchill to take pictures, I look carefully around.

Aggressive Churchill bears end up locked inside a former military hangar. And now and then, on crisp and clear afternoons, they are given an extraordinary dose of something to relax them and helicoptered far from town.

Before our tour group heads to the airport, we get to see a deeply slumbering bear as he is stretched out into a hammock-like net, winched up by the copter, and swung up high and swaying, into the blue-black arctic dome.

"Calm Air," is what I say to myself. Calm air.

The bear and I — both — are flying peacefully today. We are going home.

Peter Mandel is an author of books for children including the new "Zoo Ah-Choooo" (Holiday House), "Jackhammer Sam" (Macmillan) and "Bun, Onion, Burger" (Simon & Schuster). A regular travel contributor to The Washington Post and The Boston Globe, he has written for Harper's, The Wall Street Journal, International Herald Tribune and Los Angeles Times. His articles have won several Lowell Thomas awards from the Society of American Travel Writers. He lives in Providence, RI. See petermandel.net.

RICHARD MCCULLOCH

DESERTED IN THE GOBI
China

It was day 48 of the greatest adventure of our lives.

"*Wo jiao* Michael," said my traveling companion, sitting in the middle of the back seat, introducing himself to our new hosts. I rolled my eyes in anticipation of what was inevitably to follow.

"Like Michael Jackson!" he said, grasping a chunk of his mangy, long hair.

"Ah!" our hosts yelped in excited recognition. "Mi'kel Jak'son!!"

This was the 55th car to pick us up and the 55th time I'd heard this comparison.

"Richard," I said, leaning forward. "*Wo jiao* Richard. Like Richard Gere?"

The three youngsters looked at each other scratching their heads. No one ever knew Richard Gere.

Hitchhike No. 55 had started like every other: The surge of elation that followed being picked up was a welcome respite from the tedium of waiting. The feeling of satisfaction that we were about to chip another tiny chuck out of the 20'000 km (12,427 miles) of road that separated us from the green pastures of Shropshire, England, had precipitated an eager thirst for information about our new hosts.

We were in the car with a trio of teenagers: a couple in the front and another boy in the back. Both the boys had a feathery adolescent mustache and the girl had her long black hair tied in a ponytail. Michael and I took turns firing questions at them from our Lonely Planet phrasebook. Every one of them was met with cries of glee from our hosts — a kind of innocent enthusiasm that never failed to affect us.

Between the questions, I took the time, as I often did, to gaze at our surroundings; a conscious attempt to absorb as many of the different landscapes as I could into my memory. It's perhaps a strange, circumscribed way to experience the world — speeding past you from behind a car window. It was as if a great Bayeux Tapestry was unraveling at 90 km per hour as we leapfrogged our way through the continent, from car to lorry to car.

From the bustling villages of Indonesia, to the futuristic cityscape of Singapore, through the vibrant jungles of Malaysia and Thailand, on the capricious twists and turns of the mountain roads in Laos, past the rice fields cast sporadically across the southern Chinese valleys, through one anonymous mega-metropolis to the next, we had reached the historic city of Xian, in the center of China. From there we journeyed northwest following the trail of the old Silk Road — the ancient network of trade, a kind of umbilical cord of commerce, connecting the great empires of West and East. What had once facilitated the exchange of everything from merchandise, culture, language, philosophy, technology and disease was now transporting us, two dusty travelers from the verdant pastures of Shropshire through the desolate wilderness of the third-largest non-polar desert in the world, the Gobi.

We had been picked up in Jiayuguan, a remote town about 628 km (390 miles) from the next site of discernible civilization, Hami. If you look at the shape of China as a chicken, we were deep in the tail feathers. The lush tropics of the South Pacific were a distant memory, and the farther we headed north and west the colder and emptier the landscape had become.

After the Great Sandy Desert in Australia, I'd say the Gobi is the second most aptly named desert in existence. Its name means "waterless place" and, indeed, it is a notoriously greedy desert with an insatiable thirst for fertile land. Just like a modern day Mongol Empire, it is expanding south, year after year, devouring as much as 3,600 km2 of grassland each time. We'd also noticed that the farther we'd headed north and west, the more the people seemed to absorb the characteristics of their environment. Up until Xian, the local people had been, at times, overwhelmingly generous, friendly and open. Since then, however, the inhabitants of colder, miserly more ruthless lands had become just that. It was with increasing frequency that drivers would demand exorbitant amounts of money to give us a ride.

We'd been in the car for about two hours and, if I was to hazard a guess, I would have said we were exactly 328 km (203 miles) from the town we'd left and 328 km from the town we're heading for. One of the joys of hitchhiking is that you're at the mercy of the whims of your host. Usually these whims pertain to generosity, friendliness or benevolence, but not always. Hitchhiking sometimes manifests the darker sides of human nature as well, as we were to soon find out.

The boy in the back had been studying the phrasebook for a while, mesmerized. Michael was similarly engaged, listening to his iPod. His hair had grown wild and unwashed, his beard like a nest of dry, ginger straw. He looks like a caveman, I thought, which in hindsight proved to be an ominous reflection. I sniffed his shoulder, which he noticed but chose to ignore. Not terrible, I remember thinking, just like athlete's foot: repugnant, that is, unless it's your own.

I suddenly realized that all three of our hosts were staring at me, even the driver. Looks of curiosity/bewilderment were ingrained in their youthful faces. We were probably the first Westerners they'd ever seen in the flesh. I decided to stop sniffing Michael's shoulder. They considered us for a few moments more, before a debate broke out between them. The couple in the front were discussing something of importance — or perhaps they were arguing. It was difficult to tell. The only thing I could count on was that the subject was us; it was obvious from the intermittent glances in the rear-view mirror.

The boy next to Michael passed him the phrasebook and Michael duly pulled out his earphones.

"Huh?" he said, as the boy pointed to a phrase. Michael read aloud the phrase, which was apparently in the shopping section of the book.

"How–much–does–it–cost?"

My attention flittered for a spit second to the other side of the highway — I thought I'd seen a car but it was merely the sun, now low in the sky ahead of us, reflecting momentarily from a sign.

"What?" said Michael, "what does what cost? My iPod?"

He'd been asked this question a few times before. The boy looked at the iPod but shook his head. He pointed to the phrase again and then gestured at the space all around us to indicate the car. I could see the driver's face in the mirror break into a grin.

"How much is the car?" asked Michael, with a knitted brow. It dawned on me what was about to happen.

"He means the ride," I said. "He means how much for the ride, the lift."

We didn't mind paying drivers for our rides sometimes. If we were in a country where it was customary to do so, the "when in Rome" motto seemed a reasonable course of action. If a fee was requested, it was usually negotiated before we got into the vehicle. We always armed ourselves with the knowledge of the price of a bus ticket between the places we were traveling and, as a general rule, if we were charged anything over that price, we rejected the offer and if it was anything below, we jumped aboard. Up until this point, 8'388 km (5,200 miles) into our journey, we'd paid for six out of 55 rides, from 2.50 pounds ($4) to 5 pounds ($8).

This time I had an uneasy feeling creeping into my stomach. It seemed like these kids had purposely waited until we were at our most vulnerable, the farthest point between where we'd started and where were going.

The boy handed Michael a notepad and gestured for him to offer a price. Michael wrote the price of a bus ticket and returned it back. The boy's eyes widened, squinted and then his eyebrows fell low. He reported the figure to the two in front. The driver snorted in disbelief. They were clearly expecting more. The girl with the long pony tail looked out her window, seemingly disinterested in the proceedings.

The driver caught my attention in the rear-view mirror and rubbed his thumb and forefinger together — the one gesture we've found to be truly international. Michael returned the notepad again and gestured for him to write a price. The boy said a few words to the driver, who muttered a reply. The girl's head jerked back around and she spat a sharp word or two at the driver.

Michael and I looked at each other as the girl continued to express her anger in rapid Chinese.

The boy in the back wrote a figure, crossed it out, thought for a few seconds, wrote another figure and passed it to Michael. Michael took a look at the number, sighed with a smile and cast his eyes to the heavens.

"What is it?" I dared to ask.

"You don't want to know," he replied earnestly. I took the notepad. The price was 100 times what we'd initially offered to pay, the equivalent of a week of our budget in China. It looked more like an international phone number. I made eye contact with the girl; she looked again out the window, not that there was much to see. We'd entered a shallow ravine, with some small, white chalky hills on either side of us. A few heavy moments of silence passed.

The driver was the first to break, clearing his throat. He made the familiar money gesture with the hand he wasn't steering with and then pointed outside into the desert. As if the ultimatum wasn't clear enough, he slowed right down then pulled over. The girl started complaining again, but the driver silenced her with an aggressive bang of his hand onto the dashboard.

I'm not sure what they expected us to do. Perhaps they were only trying to scare us into paying up. We certainly didn't have that kind of money on us – we'd have been fools to do so. Looking back, perhaps we could have given them assurances that we'd pay up in the next town or perhaps we should have attempted to negotiate a more reasonable price. These things didn't occur to us at the time.

I watched the boy in the back's jaw fall open in astonishment as I opened the car door and stepped outside. Michael shook each person's hand and thanked them with more sincerity than I could have managed had I attempted it. As they drove off, with a spin of their wheels on the dusty road, I could hear the girl screeching in high irate tones at what had just occurred. The boy in back watched us from the back window until the car disappeared into the horizon.

"What did you thank them for?" I asked Michael.

"They drove us 328 km. That's 128 km more than our daily target."

I couldn't resist smiling. Here we were, without any food or water, stranded in one of the most unforgiving environments on earth. While we'd been driving, deeper and deeper into this barren wasteland of a place, we hadn't seen a single vehicle on either side of the road. We only had a few hours of sunlight left and the temperatures were reputed to drop to as low as minus 40. I couldn't help but admire and envy Michael's positivity.

The air felt cold in our lungs and loud on our breath as we walked toward the sun, which was perhaps a couple of hours away from settling down for the night behind the horizon. We'd left the plateau and had now dropped with the road into a mini-valley, with low, chalky hills on either side of us. Despite being barren and largely featureless, our surroundings, cast perfectly in the silent winter sunset, possessed a stark, extra-terrestrial kind of beauty.

After another two hours passed, the feelings of hunger were gnawing at our stomachs, the cold was seeping into our bones and tiredness whittling away at our morale.

"Well, on the plus side," Michael said, surveying the valley with a somewhat studious look on his face. "I've started to see quite a few caves around."

We continued walking for about 30 seconds as his words hung in the air.

"Yes," he continued, "from time to time I've often thought about what we should do if we ever find ourselves in a situation like this. We should sleep back-to-back, to keep our backs warm, while our arms keep our fronts warm"

"Good thinking Michael," I agreed, pretending that I hadn't just had a somewhat startling vision of me killing him, eating his flesh, burning his corpse for warmth and then dancing around the cave with the charred remains of his skeleton for a laugh.

"What are you grinning at Rich?"

"Oh errr... nothing," I chuckled. "Hey, do you hear something?"

We heard the faintest of rumblings behind us and turned around. In any other landscape on earth such a distant sound would have been absorbed into the scenery or ignored by the occupants, but here even our hearts sounded like drums in our chests. Squinting into the distance, with the sun behind us, we saw a sparkle of reflected light. To say it was like how a sailor, marooned for days on a raft at sea, would react to the sight of land would be an exaggeration. Perhaps our feelings were more akin to a puppy's when its owner returns from a day at work.

"A car! A car! A car!" we whimpered, skipping about. The excitement quickly turned to anxiety, however, at the thought that nothing was guaranteed. This was the first car we'd seen since the trio of teenagers that had picked us up – four hours and 300 km (186 miles) ago. Surely, I thought to myself, two random Westerners in the desert, 328 km from civilization, would be a compelling enough sight to stop!

Perhaps with the image of my malevolent, cannibalistic grin still fresh in his mind, Michael cast aside any feelings of inhibition and he stepped out of the hard shoulder and onto the highway. With the brazen pride of a showgirl at a boxing match, he held the sign for our next destination, "Hami," high above his head. I joined him by his side and I summoned from within the depths of my soul the most pitiful look of pleading sorrow that I could muster – my lip quivered, my eyes bulged and swelled with water, my knees shivered and my hands were clasped together in prayer. It was no show. I wanted to leave.

The closer and closer our savior approached, the more and more our excitement grew, and the more we shuffled out onto the highway.

"Is he slowing down?" I asked Michael, squinting my focus more tightly.

"I think so!"

And, sure enough, the car was slowing down.

There is nothing in this world that intensifies the feelings of hunger, tiredness, boredom, isolation and loneliness more than giving someone the opportunity of respite and then taking it away again. To misquote a man a lot more intelligent than I: "Hope is as good a breakfast as false hope is a bad supper."

And true these words proved to be. The car slowed down as it passed, stared at us as if we were animals in a zoo, before speeding off again, roaring like thunder, into the horizon

"Damn!" Michael shouted, throwing the sign into the dust.

"That was it," I said, kicking a stone. "That was our chance."

"Well, do you want the good news or the bad news?" he asked me.

"The good news."

"I can see a good cave."

"The bad news?"

"It's a cave."

As we turned from the road, dejected and tired, the thought of the night to come sent a small chill down my spine and the first real thoughts of concern wandered into my mind.

How long will it be before we see another car? How long will it be before another car stops? How long will it be before we can eat again? How cold will it be when the sun falls behind the horizon? Will Michael notice if I steal his scarf?

Not for the first time on our journey I was thankful not to be alone and my thoughts turned to comfort.

Which dusty rock would make a good pillow? Which dusty rock would make a good blanket? Which dusty rock could I brush my teeth with in the morning?

"I don't believe it," Michael said, breaking my train of thought.

"Huh?" I replied.

"Another car is coming."

I turned around and, sure enough, he was right. No yelps of excitement or skipping around this time, however. The bitter taste of disappointment was still too fresh in our mouths. This time it was serious; now or never. We walked right out into the middle of the road and, for the first time on our hitchhiking adventure, I think the driver had to stop out of necessity rather than choice. The car slowed down, maneuvered around us, and then stopped in the hard shoulder ahead of us. We jogged up to the window and, as it opened, a thick plume of cigarette smoke oozed from within. Two pairs of masculine eyes were just about visible, peering at us through the sauna-like haze. Michael pointed at his sign. They shared a few words together then gestured for us to join them.

I let the familiar wave of elation wash over me as I slid into the back seat alongside my friend. However, whereas usually the feeling was a euphoric affirmation that the highs of hitchhiking around the world outweigh the lows, this time it was more like relief.

"*Ni hao!*" said Michael, leaning forward. "*Wo jiao* Michael. Like Michael Jackson!"

The driver looked at his friend and they both giggled in mutual recognition.

"Ah ha ha! Mik-el Jak-son!"

"The hair!" Michael said, grasping a chunk, and they all laughed some more.

"Ni hao" I said, leaning forward. "*Wo jiao* Richard. Like Richard Gere."

They stopped laughing and scratched their heads. No one ever knew Richard Gere.

In 2011, Richard McCulloch and his best friend Mike attempted to hitchhike from Australia to England, 20´000 km (12,427 miles) through 20 countries, in just 100 days. The adventures of The Rich Mike Hitch Hike are documented at www.therichmikehitchhike.com.

CLAIRE IBARRA

IN RUINS
Peru

I woke up to another round of rooster calls. When I stuck my head out of the tent, it was just light enough to make out the silhouette of a large bull grazing on the wet, tall grass. The air was cold and damp, and normally I would have found it invigorating. That morning it was threatening, a reminder of the discomforts and hardships I would encounter throughout the day.

My body was not going to cooperate with the chilly dampness seeping into my bones, not that it had been cooperating much in the past three days. My stiff and sore muscles made climbing out of the tent too difficult. I needed to use the hole in the ground they called an outhouse, but I was good as crippled. Instead of venturing out, I snuggled back into my sleeping bag, pulling the silky nylon fabric over my head.

I groaned when I felt my husband toss and then sit up. He was the morning person, always ready to take on the world even with a hangover and embedded 21 miles into a wilderness canyon, with 20,000-foot-tall snow-capped Andean peaks surrounding us. We were camped on an Andean terrace within the Choquequirao ruins in Peru, and I myself felt thoroughly ruinous: a person ready to crumble and fall away, not to be excavated any time soon.

While listening to the rustles and whispers of our expedition members emerging from tents, I took a moment to reflect on how we had gotten there, to that moment, exhausted and rallying each other to meet the challenges of the day.

*****

I had to go back six months, when my sister-in-law died at age 38. As a single mom, she left behind two boys for her own mother to rear alone. I was filled with sadness, whereas my husband was filled with anger and a consuming grief. After having already lost his father and a brother at young ages, Oscar was having a hard time accepting, not only his sister's death, but all the implications that came along with it. A genetic heart condition was snatching away his family members one by one.

I consider myself to be a loyal person, but I can also be impatient with others. *Just pull yourself together*, I thought to myself, when I saw Oscar crushed by his loss, weighted down by fears. After months of depression, our marriage seemed to be teetering. The thing that scared me the most was the spiraling loss of control — something I still carry from my parents' divorce.

When Oscar proposed a trip to Peru, I was relieved that he was showing signs of moving on.

When he told me about his idea to trek a remote section of the Inca Trail to newly discovered ruins along the Salkantay mountain range, following the Apurimac River, I was intrigued. Yet, I couldn't possibly foresee how the vast, wild nature of the Andes would affect him. How it would release his own feral nature, and how I would temporarily lose him to it. We were adventurers. Though as weeks of planning ensued, I became wary.

Our group was taking shape and it was comprised of 11 people, including our daughters and my father. As it turned out, I was the only adult female, along with a cousin, out of the entire ragtag group. This would become a significant detail later on.

"How are we going to do this?" I asked Oscar nervously. "How do we even find our way to these ruins?" There were no roads, only a narrow trail of switchbacks following the steep and jagged Apurimac Canyon, one of the deepest canyons in the world.

"My uncle knows a local guy there (whose) family has lived in Cachora for generations," Oscar said. They organize tours, with a guide, porters and mules, tents, everything."

It sounded reasonable enough. We would depart from Cachora, a remote Indian village, and walk and camp along the trail.

Our group convened in Abancay, a small city in the Andes, after several hours of driving through mountainous, winding roads from Cuzco. We had a meeting with Nemesio that same day.

My first impression of Nemesio was good. He came to our meeting wearing a crisp white dress shirt, so different from the local Indian regalia. He was tall and slender, and dare I say dapper, even handsome? He reminded me of an Indian version of George Hamilton. He took out a notebook and pen.

"Eleven people?" he asked in a professional tone. He wrote furiously in his little notebook. "You only need to bring your food. We have a cook who will prepare it for you, and we have everything else you'll need."

"You'll provide cooking ware, pots, a propane stove, plates, utensils?" I asked. I was concerned with every detail.

"Yes, everything." He repeated this several times during the course of our conversation, where I nearly badgered him and he deflected all of my concerns with a white, brilliant George Hamilton smile.

Next stop was the market to get food to last four days for 11 people. Our camping food consisted of things like fruit, crackers, cookies, boxed juices, coffee, cans of tuna and dry pasta. Not much different than a run-of-the-mill camping trip.

The first morning we set out, our expedition was quite a spectacle. Our group of 11 had doubled in size with the porters, and, adding the mules and cargo, we looked like something from another era — when people traveled long distances in elaborate caravans. We were energetic and excited.

The trail would be fairly smooth for the first leg, made easier by the zigzagging switchbacks. Starting out that morning, Nemesio was in control of the situation, ordering the Indian porters around with an air of machismo and authority. I knew the culture well enough not to be offended.

He rambled to Oscar about the Apus mountain gods. Like most indigenous cultures, the Incas worshipped creatures, objects and forces in nature. The mountain gods, the Apus, were ubiquitous and also mysterious. Over the course of the day, Nemesio insisted upon ceremonial prayers and rituals at every lookout point.

He and Oscar would stand facing one another with their hands in prayer position, as Nemesio recited in Quechua. But it also seemed, as the day wore on, that Nemesio became increasingly belligerent and unpredictable. It wasn't until the afternoon that I realized he was completely drunk.

Apparently, the ceremonial ritual involved pouring moonshine onto the sacred earth, but mostly it required swigging it down. The ceremony was just a ruse for getting plastered. My husband had gone along for the ride.

At one open, flat lookout that gave us a view of the entire mountain range, Nemesio and Oscar began their ritual. They stood facing one another, and I watched as Nemesio removed the Indian scarf from his neck and placed it around Oscar's. The gesture looked like a priestly sacrament.

We were hours into the hike along the wilderness canyon. The rocky trail was becoming narrow and steep. I watched Oscar run and slide off the trail and into the brush, only to emerge jumping onto boulders and pounding his chest. He'd leap off again, disappearing for long stretches, but I could hear his howling and mad laughter all around us.

This was to remain his state of being and state of mind for the rest of the journey.

Looking back, I believe he was purging anger and desperation for his sister's death, for the genetic condition that could have taken him as well. Nemesio remained drunk for the rest of the trip, without an apparent excuse.

The rocky trail became treacherous and dangerous by that afternoon, as we made our way down to the river. Mules carried the group down, slipping occasionally on rocks only to catch their footing at the last minute, facing an abyss merely inches away. It was a sheer cliff down to the river.

Our meal during the day had consisted of dry snacks and fruit. We munched on granola bars, oranges, apples, and crackers with peanut butter spread. Once the camp was set up that evening, I realized our newest predicament.

The two men in charge, Nemesio and Oscar, were still drunk. So Nemesio's brother, Pedro, was in charge by default. Pedro was an older gentleman, who wore a straw hat and chewed on coca leaves. He was tall and lanky, quiet and mild-mannered. He had been fairly elusive the entire day, but now I called on him for help.

When I asked him to set up the stove and help get the food ready, he handed me a large pot. That was it. He handed me the pot and stared at me blankly.

"Are you going to help prepare the food for us? Nemesio said your tour included a cook to make the meals," I said. Again, he stared at me blankly and shrugged. He strolled off, without further explanation. I limped around in confusion, my body already going into shock from the demanding eight-hour hike.

After further investigation, I found out that not only did we not have someone to help cook for our large group, but also there were no plates, no utensils, no stove, no pans, nothing. There was only one large pot.

I marched, though really I limped, up to Nemesio, who was passed out on a plastic tarp. I shook him awake, and began yelling, "This is unacceptable. The group has to eat, and you are going to build a campfire right now." He lurched up and disappeared into a wooded area.

I climbed into my tent and began to cry. When my daughters crawled into the tent, and asked me what was wrong, I lied. "Everything is fine, girls. I'm just sore from the walk."

The girls were both stoic, refusing to complain. My dad sensed something was wrong, but mostly was lost in translation, and he had his own worries with the physical demands of the day.

From my tent, I yelled out to my female companion, "Ingue, what are we going to feed the kids? What should we do?"

From her own tent, a few feet away, I heard her moan and then say, "Who cares? Let them eat crackers."

Nemesio reappeared some time later with twigs for a fire. Stones were placed around it, to rest the pot on. Once the water was boiling, I threw in the pasta, then added tuna and salad dressing. Voila!

I watched as Nemesio conversed sternly with the Indian porters standing in a semi-circle around our group a short distance away. Their shadowy forms seemed ghostly.

I couldn't decipher what he said, but one of the Indians slowly and reluctantly handed a large plastic trash bag to Nemesio. He opened it and began passing out battered tin and plastic plates, utensils and cups to our group.

I asked Pedro, "We're using their dishes?"

"Sí, Mamá."

"You didn't bring any for our group?"

"Nemesio forgot, Mamá."

My face burned with shame. It felt rude to be taking from them. But then as we began to eat, I noticed something else.

"Pedro, what are the porters going to eat?"

"I don't know, Mamá."

"Don't you provide their food?" I already knew where this was headed, even as I asked the question.

"We don't usually feed them. That's OK, they're used to it." Pedro scratched at the dirt with his walking stick, refusing to meet my gaze. My heart sank again.

The porters still stood in the same spot, a short distance away in a semi-circle, watching us with serious but kind expressions. They watched as we ate from their own plates and forks. Oscar was alert to the situation now, and he announced that we would share our food with them. And, of course, that was the right thing to do.

As each person finished, they passed the plates and forks over, and I dished out the tuna pasta concoction. And somehow, like loaves and fishes, there was plenty to go around. And that was how it would be for the next three days: miracle after miracle in that there was always just enough, though we had doubled our numbers.

That night, Oscar proudly showed me the red woven scarf he had received as a gift from Nemesio.

"He told me that the scarf was woven by his great-great-grandmother. Look at the details in the design." Oscar passed me the scarf, as he continued, "It's been in their family for generations, but he wanted me to have it."

It looked aged and worn, and it was beautifully woven with patterns in yellow, blue and green. It did seem to be a generous and special gift. Oscar wouldn't take it off.

By the second day, we were dusty, sore and tired, but we kept our spirits up. We crossed a narrow suspension bridge over the raging river. The rapids below were white and foamy. Making our way up the other side of the canyon would be as treacherous as it had been going down.

Nemesio continued his ritual to the Apus gods, with Oscar in tow wearing his beloved Indian scarf. In the evenings, we were on the search for dry twigs for the fire, since we had entered a damp, semi-tropical ecosystem and all the foliage was wet. But our pot served us well, and apparently was sufficient to keep us from starving, and for making coffee in the mornings. We took turns and shared the pot with the porters; they don't drink coffee but rather coca leaf tea.

One evening, I asked Pedro to find twigs for the fire, and he looked pensively up at the starry sky. He searched there silently for a long while, pacing along the grassy pasture with his head lifted toward the heavens. Did he find his twigs up there in the vast night sky? I would never know. Our nephews became experts though, coming to camp loaded with branches of every size.

We had set up camp inside the archeological site of the Choquequirao ruins.

I was bone tired, and resigned to being dirty and sore and frustrated by the lack of organization. When it was dinnertime, I felt like shouting out, "Let them eat cake!" but, once again, there was a miracle feast before us.

I came to an odd sort of peace with Nemesio. By our last night, I had accepted his incompetence as just part of the experience.

We sat together, watching our campfire, not glowing brightly but rather billowing endless clouds of thick, gray smoke from the dampness, as the noodles boiled. I said, "Nemesio, can I give you one suggestion for your future tours? It would really help to have a propane stove for a group this large."

"Oh, I have one, Mamá, I just didn't bring it."

"Why not?" I asked, flabbergasted.

"It's more authentic this way," he told me.

But there we were. With all the tears, sweat, and pain, it was magical. We were in the middle of the citadel, surrounded by artful stone masonry and lush vegetation, and the moon shone brightly so we could explore and discover rock walls and secret steps throughout the grounds. There were no other tourists. We were smack dab in the middle of pristine nature and a wondrous history. Not long after our trip, camping was restricted at the site by the government.

Once we arrived back in the village of Cachora, one of the porters shyly approached my husband. The porter hunched slightly, keeping his head and eyes downcast.

Nearly in a whisper the porter asked, "I'm sorry but can I have my scarf back now?"

"This is your scarf?" Oscar asked in disbelief.

"Nemesio took it from me."

Oscar offered a more than generous sum and the porter happily sold it to him.

But the story doesn't end there.

Do you think we simply went home to retell the story at dinner parties, of how we survived Nemesio the Drunk? Or how Oscar conquered his internal struggles, winning the battle with his demons to eventually find peace with life and death itself?

A year later, we bought a property in the Indian village of Cachora. We constructed a rustic, quaint hostel and began to organize our own tours to the ruins.

Claire Ibarra is a writer and photographer who lives in Miami. Her work has appeared in "Pure Slush: Travel Stories," "Roadside Fiction" and "Alimentum —The Literature of Food," among many other journals and magazines. She and her husband own a hostel in Cachora, a small village in the Andes of Peru en route to the Choquequirao ruins. You can learn more at claireibarra.com

BRUCE NORTHAM

THE NAKED TRUTH
New Guinea

"It is an interesting question how far men would retain their relative rank if they were divested of their clothes."
—Thoreau, Walden 1854

Sledding to the Poles, summiting Everest, rowing across an ocean…it's all been done before. However, in an age when earthbound pioneer glory is virtually unattainable, I slid into a premiere — playing naked Frisbee with Stone Age natives. Someone had to do it.

Simplicity died when fashion was born. What is it about modern culture that feels the need to impose a foreign language, a way of life and a religion on a people who live in communion deep in an impenetrable forest? The well-intended but often genocidal influence of outsiders continues as Irian Jayan highland tribes, guilty only of nudity, succumb to an alien oppression. One force driving this Aboriginal extermination is that frontiersman psychology.

Irian Jaya makes up half of New Guinea, the world's second-largest island. This Melanesian holdout is Indonesia's least-populated territory, and nothing like Bali. Torrential rivers plunge from the peaks into gorges and lush lowland rainforests before flowing out toward the coastal plains. Even today, representatives of tribes unknown to the outside world periodically emerge from the forests. In 1990, a previously unidentified group surfaced. Ambassadors of the tribe, evidently shocked by what they saw, immediately disappeared again.

Accessible only by air or after a month of hacking through a steamy jungle with a machete, the Baliem Valley was my launch point for a month-long trek into the region's highlands, requiring a blend of valley walking, high-endurance climbing and cliff scaling. The rugged terrain isolates intimate Dani tribe villages, which are segmented by stone fences and surrounded by sweet-potato vine gardens, canals and steep, terraced mountainsides.

The walking routes are the natives' prolific trade trail system. Occasionally, I pull over to let trios of bow-and-arrow toting hunters pass. Mud abounds. You haven't officially trekked until you've had a boot sucked off by a foot of mud — never a concern for the barefoot Dani. In fact, the dark-skinned Afro-resembling Melanesian Aborigines still wear only penis gourds, an early-model jock strap made from petrified yellow squash shells that are fitted over their genitalia and fastened skyward by thin strings tied around the waist. The old-style way to rock it.

Ruuf, my Dani guide for the first leg of my trek, led me, calm, wise and barefoot, leaping nimbly from slippery log to log. When I lost him, I tracked his mud prints. A long, grass-mesh bilum bag slung around his forehead and draped across his back contained sweet potatoes, compressed tobacco, leaves for rolling cigarettes and a small bag of salt. His primordial briefcase also toted a palm-leaf mat doubling as a rain poncho. Upon his head, it resembled a nun's habit.

Unsuspected downpours are common, and one monsoon shower was especially enlightening. Betrayed by flooded boots and soaked by sweat inside my raingear, I caught Ruuf smiling under his temporal tepee with not even a drop of water on his petrified squash. Pausing there in the downpour, I contemplated my departure from the essential laws of human survival, a defeated poster child of Western survival gear. I was seduced into surrendering to my innermost nomadic calling — the contents of my backpack later becoming gifts. Luxuries are often not only hindrances but also dispensable.

En route, we encountered 20 local men resting on a bluff overlooking a terraced valley and the thundering Baliem River. The shoeless posse was hauling supplies to their village 30 miles away. Suddenly, they broke into a three-part harmony a cappella, an ancestral call to unite and energize the group. Their simple spirit-lifting chant reminded me of the feeling you get when a bird or other animals hop over and sits by you in the forest — date and time momentarily wait. Sublime.

Ruuf and I shared many bowls of rice. We nibbled small fingersfull, caveman-like, and peered about the forest. I heard bird calls, Ruuf heard food. I showed him a photo of a girlfriend. Mixing pantomime with intonation, I attempted to inquire, "Have you ever seen the sea? He shook his head no. "What is your favorite food?" He pointed toward sweet potatoes. "What do you dream about?" He glanced down at the photo of the blonde woman and grinned wide. Archetypal humor.

People are usually more complex than what initial impressions may convey. Frequently, one of the first questions upon meeting someone is "What do you do?" which is often misconstrued as who you are. How would Ruuf answer this question? We'll never know. The man for all seasons and I parted with a prehistoric handshake, lasting a minute, graduating to a mutual bicep shake, and adjourning with condoning nods. I headed for a nap in a village dwelling, and he ran off, in the buff and into his boondocks.

*****

Indonesian officials have failed in getting all of the inhabitants of this "wild east" to support "Operation Penis Gourd," which is designed to get them out of their traditional getup and into Western clothing. When these seniors pass on, this sartorial tradition and much of their old way of living will be history. Wave goodbye to the Stone Age and hello to naked shame.

It's difficult to process the rugged, simple beauty of these formerly fierce headhunters and cannibals who discarded stone axes for steel in the mid-1900s. Clock time remains irrelevant here. The small, wiry women do most of the chores, such as raising the children, pigs and sweet potatoes. They often lug up to 80 pounds of potatoes, and a baby, for miles up and down steep mountain trails. Women work the fields, while the men generally walk around, chat, pose for photos and smoke cigarettes. Intrepid prototypes indeed. The men also tend the squash-to-be-gourds, which they manipulate to grow according to the shape of the manhood sheath they fancy. I tried on a few gourds in various villages, which eventually led me to a new level of embarrassment.

Living in tidy, wood-thatched, grass-domed huts called *honays*, men and women sleep and pass time in separate two-story huts. I was permitted to sleep, and reflect, in *honays* after receiving consent from a village chief. Certain bungalows are the privilege of men who've established themselves as warriors. A tad rustic, if you focus on the fleas and mice, these alpha-male sanctuaries are fertile pastures for the imagination — superstitiously invested shrunken animal heads, spears, weaponry and charms hang from the roofs.

The Dani converse in soft tones, if they speak at all. Illuminated by a well-tended fire, we sat in a circle, puffing clove cigarettes, noshing on warm sweet potatoes, enveloped in smoke. Imitating the dudes, I inhaled the clove deeply and achieved a serene cannabis euphoria. Knee-deep in nomadic caché, I accepted the silence as meditation, in a corner of the world where safety pins were once fair trade for a shrunken human head. Meanwhile, the reigning thought in my mind during the interlude was Einstein's prophesy about not being sure about the outcome of a third world war, but asserting that the fourth world war would be fought with sticks and stones. Surely, these vanguards would endure, in spite of pressure to get online with the global economy.

I spent the next morning in church, a wooden cabin with a corrugated tin roof, packed with quasi-clad worshippers. Women and girls sat on the left side, men and boys sat on the right. A lonely dead-battery clock loomed above a makeshift wood box altar, behind it the rambling missionary preacher was the only other person wearing clothes. Seated beside me was a man wearing only a chunky beige gourd, a band of greasy chicken feathers on his head, and a clove cigarette stored in his earlobe piercing.

Patiently waiting to interact with the preacher, he inserted a quarter-moon-shaped pig bone into his pierced nasal septum. Although lost on me, their discussion enraptured everyone else. The women sat quietly with netlike bilum bags slung around their heads, bulging with provisions and babies. An unsympathetic gatekeeper declined to let people leave before the service concluded.

During prayer, all eyes were closed and heads lowered. Interestingly, they cover both eyes with one hand during prayers in fear of going blind. First came the peek-a-boo glances at the peculiar albino, then the restrained library chuckling. When the service ended, the women passed me to exit the church, their handshakes missing digits. I learned that the older women cut off one or several finger joints as part of a cremation ceremony when someone in their immediate family passes on. Some women I met were missing most of their fingers. Severing a corner of the earlobe is the corresponding practice for men.

Bartering also enthuses the Dani. Safety pins remain a prevailing souvenir trade item. They have become their all-in-one toolbox: surgical implement, fishhook, necklace ornament, wood etcher, earring and so on. Velcro also makes a splash. Purchasing 6-foot-long hunting arrows was one task, getting them through airport security and onto eight different connecting U.S.-bound planes was another. I still use the custom-fit gourd I smuggled home as a prop in my keynote presentation.

In "Walden," Thoreau speaks of a "realometer," a raw, instinctive gauge to rate the wow-factor of our individual convictions. Here, my realometer stayed pinned to the max. Likewise, foreign visitors can astonish these natives. My icebreaker was also my contribution: a Frisbee. They were riveted by this simple aircraft, a pie-tin cum UFO. The flying saucer captured their imagination and made them belly laugh. Initially, I was concerned that by introducing this game, I was further adding to the ruination of a traditional way of life that deserved to be preserved. My first instinct went against introducing a non-neutral item into their culture, but unanimous child happiness cemented the verdict, and it isn't difficult to replicate a disc using preexisting items — their circular rattan "place mats," we discovered, also flew. At this time, there was still a standing back-flip in my public entertainment arsenal, and each village ranked it up there with making things fly.

While other tradition-defying forces impose religion and outlander value, I tossed my neon-blue flying disc into the last primeval frontier, and they rejoiced wildly over it. Upon entering a small village, I'd stroll into an open area, usually the courtyard in the midst of the hut complex, and spin the Sputnik so it hovered and descended gradually into the waiting huddle. Some ran to it, some ran from it and kept on running. It was perhaps the biggest single event to hit these villages since the first invader donated matches. Now, that's Ultimate Frisbee. The Papua natives, having developed for millennia in isolation, have many unique traits including a hunting talent for throwing and launching spears. Straightaway, many of the younger Frisbee throwers advanced from having never seen one to being able to wing it 200 feet — using unconventional gripping techniques, or launching it upside-down.

I played sort of nude, too. At first my gourd was a discomfiture; some of us wage a continuing struggle against fashion. The string tied around my waist failed to hold up the hardened vegetable case that kept fumbling downward, and it itched. I didn't like sprinting barefoot across rocky fields, and I was paranoid about injuring my exposed nutsack. I concluded that some of them intentionally tossed the Frisbee astray, so I'd have to run for it. They laughed at that too.

*****

Clothing optional might be optimal. The Dani, former cannibals, seem like the most gentle and hospitable people on earth. Thoreau suggested that people are rich in proportion to the number of things they can afford to let alone. Too bad we can't let this final pristine refuge be. In a surge of serendipity, a culture that doesn't bother to keep track of its age adopted one harmless result of the times — flying plastic.

It will be some time before Frisbees rival the importance of pigs in this quiet corner of the world. Near the end of my sojourn back in time, I entered a village and pitched the flying disc into another curious horde. This village chief had difficulty catching, throwing and comprehending it, as did some of the other elders. His discontent with the game grew when the disobedient aircraft drifted into the pigpen, spooking the priceless swine. The chief abruptly disappeared into the men's *honay*.

As the sun was setting and the Frisbee fanfare was winding down, the chief reappeared. Strutting erect, bows and arrows slung across his back, he paused in the center of the village and drew an arrow. Focusing, he aimed skyward at the hovering disc. A second later the Frisbee's heart was punctured. Crippled, it wobbled to earth. Justice. My realometer flared. Game over, the chief retrieved the impaled UFO and retired into his hut.

The wind whistled through my gourd.

Bruce Northam is an award-winning journalist and author of "Globetrotter Dogma," "In Search of Adventure" and "The Frugal Globetrotter." He is also the creator of "American Detour," a show detailing the travel writer's journey. His keynote speech, "Directions to Your Destination," reveals many shades of the travel industry, including how to entice travelers. Northam's other live presentation, "Street Anthropology," is an ode to freestyle wandering. His website is americandetour.com.

JANNA GRABER

FILLING IN THE HOLES
Latvia

For some reason, I had always imagined it smaller, but the river that took my family is wide and beautiful. As powerful as the Mississippi, the mighty Daugava River runs from western Russia through Belarus and into Latvia before draining into an arm of the Baltic Sea.

Right here, where I stand, the Daugava pushes against the wide river banks of Riga, the Latvian capital. On one side lies medieval Old Town Riga, with its ancient cathedrals, tidy cobblestone alleys and Art Nouveau treasures. Across the bridge – a modern design that could be in any European city – lies the Riga of today, with offices, shops, apartments and even the ultra-modern Latvian National Library, which opened in 2014.

It has taken my family almost 100 years to return to this land, this tiny nation on the Baltic Sea – and for right now, it is just me, gathering in all I can of Latvia and its people, trying to pick up the pieces of what was lost here.

*****

Mention Latvia and many people will scratch their heads. Little is known about this country of 2 million just across the sea from Sweden and bordering Estonia, Lithuania, Russia and Belarus. With a language and culture all their own, Latvians have lived here quietly for centuries. But invading nations, from the Swedes to the Russians to the Germans, have often sought to take Latvia for their own. All too often, in the last hundred years, Latvians have been caught in the middle.

My grandfather was one of them.

He was just 14 years old in 1915 when rumors began to swirl about Germans invading Latvia. At first, people weren't concerned. Like most good Latvians, my grandpa and his family spent their summers in the countryside. Though they lived in Riga during the school year, when the warm weather came, his mother packed up the kids and off they went to the family farm.

At the time, Latvia had already been claimed by Russia, and advancing German soldiers could only mean trouble. As Germans began to fill the countryside, my family decided it was time to flee. The older teenage sons, fearing conscription, were sent north. My grandfather and his sisters accompanied his mom as they packed up some of the family belongings. My grandfather was tasked with bringing along a pair of sheep.

They joined hundreds of refugees, often sleeping in abandoned castles or fields as they slowly walked toward Riga. Finally, they reached the Daugava River, and the refugees lined up to cross the bridge. But just as my grandfather and his family began to cross, the Germans began shelling.

In the chaos, my grandfather ended up in the river. He couldn't swim, but the sheep could. He finally made it safely to the shore.

I think about that now, as I look at the river. My whole family line saved by a pair of sheep.

When he fell into the river, my grandpa was separated from his family. He waited all day on the river banks, hoping to find them, but they never appeared. He spent days searching, but found no one. Did his family die in the river? Were their bodies swept out to sea? Or was his mother searching frantically for her child only to keep missing him?

He never found them. As he said once many years later, he started across the bridge that day with his family and ended up on the other side completely alone. Although I never got to meet my grandpa (he died when I was a baby), I had been told that story since I was a child. Yet I had never really understood that loss until now.

I wonder why on earth it took me so long to get here.

*****

My heart had been beating a mile a minute when my boyfriend Ben and I arrived in Riga. My eyes were glued to the window as we flew in from Stockholm and then took a taxi into town. It felt like I was going to meet a long-lost old relative, someone I had heard about, but was very nervous to meet.

The first thing I had wanted to see was the river – the river where everything had changed for my family. So here I am now, still standing on the river banks. I try to imagine that tragic day. But it is hard to think of such tragedy when the sun is shining and there is a beautiful European city waiting to be explored. So Ben and I turn around and head back into Old Town.

Named a UNESCO World Heritage site, Old Town Riga has been carefully restored and preserved. Not a speck of trash can be seen on the streets, and most of the buildings have fresh coats of paint, many in pale yellows, blues, greens and ochre.

We've chosen to stay at Old Riga Hotel Vecriga, a tiny boutique property in the heart of Old Town. The price of 150 euros a night includes full breakfast and dinner for two, and we can walk to all the main attractions. Latvia is one of the last affordable destinations in Europe.

After dropping off our things, we set off eagerly to explore. I can't help feeling a bit giddy as we turn down corner after corner, for Riga is more beautiful than I had imagined. I knew that Latvia had been in the grip of communism for decades and had only recently become part of the European Union, but I hadn't know how far it had come.

Latvia gained its independence in 1991 after "The Baltic Way," a powerful peaceful protest in 1989 when 2 million people across the three Baltic countries of Latvia, Lithuania and Estonia stood hand in hand in a human chain to protest Soviet rule. The chain spanned more than 600km, and it affirmed their unity and expressed their yearning for freedom. The event began the path toward independence in all three Baltic nations after the fall of the totalitarian Soviet regime.

That independence looks good on this small country of determined people. The cobblestone streets of Old Town have the look of a tidy Swiss village, but with a flair all their own. The outdoor patios of the restaurants are lined with flower boxes and filled to the brim with patrons.

*****

Riga was declared the European Capital of Culture for 2014. The town is pulsing with young life, and while capitalism here is alive and well, I don't see the gaudy look of visible Western greed.

Our first stop is at an outdoor café for coffee and pastries. As we lounge in the sun, I enjoy people-watching. Many of the Latvians are blond and blue-eyed. I also see many wide Russian faces; a quarter of Latvia's population is Russian.

I can't help but notice that most Latvians are slim and fit. Western overindulgence doesn't seem to have reached Latvia yet. As I study the women who walk by, many of whom are wearing pretty summer dresses with sensible heels, I am struck by something – they are of medium height, but are small-boned with tiny waists, like me.

For years, the women in my family have struggled to find clothes in America that fit. Almost every skirt or pair of pants that I buy has to be tailored at the waist. But here, I see that many women have my same frame. I test out my theory later in the afternoon by going shopping. Sure enough – I find many items that fit. I go into four stores and come out with several bags full of clothing that fit like a glove.

While shopping and later dining out, I'm surprised at the level of English I find in Riga. Though most people were forced to learn Russian in the Soviet days, every shop keeper, waiter and hotel personnel we've met has spoken English with ease. It's impressive for a country that only opened up to the western world in 1991.

The day goes by quickly, and we're shocked to look at our watches and find that it's almost 10 p.m. The sun is still shining. Northern winters may be hard, but summers in the far north offer long days of sunshine. Those days are something to be celebrated, and the streets are still filled with families, couples and friends out enjoying the warm summer air. We join everyone else and relax in one of the many town squares for a late dinner, listening to live music.

All these years, Latvia had always been a foggy blur in my mind. Yet here it is – alive, thriving and absolutely beautiful. Part of me feels like skipping all the way back to our hotel.

*****

Latvia today is a vibrant part of the European Union, but that independence was long in coming. Soon after he lost his family in 1915, my grandpa was deported or fled to Russia, along with 700,000 other Latvians. He ended up in Siberia, where he found himself in the middle of the growing Russian Revolution and was forced to fight with the White Russians.

Tired and weary, he made his way across Russia and to a refugee camp in the Philippines. After hopping a sea freighter, he eventually washed up on the shores of California at the age of 19. He picked a new last name from the phone book and took odd jobs. Finally, he joined the U.S. Army Air Corps, where he spent the rest of his career.

WWII would take him back to Europe as an American soldier, but Latvia, though so close, was unreachable. After WWII, the Soviets locked Latvia behind the Iron Curtain.

How often he must have wondered about his family. I wonder about them now, too. Do I still have family here?

Being here in Latvia, I finally understand the mark that war can leave on a family for generations. It's a story that has occurred in many families – parents flee, leaving a country and culture behind. They try so hard to survive in the new country that there is little energy to remember what was left behind. All those traditions, family, friends, foods, beloved places and even language are lost. But they often leave a hole, even if the following generations don't know it.

The hole that was left behind in my grandfather was filled with silence. He married later in life and had children in his 40s. By all accounts, he was a quiet man who rarely spoke, rarely engaged at all, leaving his three children grappling on their own to find their confidence. He never spoke his language again, and rarely spoke of that day he lost everything in Riga. Fortunately, he told his story once on tape, capturing it for later generations to hear.

Ambiguous loss – not knowing what has happened to someone you have lost – leaves a deep hole. Parents who have had a child disappear have felt it. Those whose loved ones were on the unfortunate Malaysia Airlines 370 that disappeared in 2014 felt it. And now I realize that my grandfather must have felt it, too.

*****

I'm hoping to learn as much about Latvia as I can. Culture can dilate over generations, and often the only remnants that survive can be found in food and holiday traditions.

I start with the food. From the few stories I've heard about my grandpa, I know that he liked to eat pickled fish and dark bread. Pickled vegetables were also a common household staple.

Ben and I discover whole aisles of pickled and smoked fish, as well as dark breads at Riga's Central Market. Housed in five former Zeppelin hangers that the Germans left behind, it is one of the largest farmer's markets in Europe. The aisles of each hanger are overflowing with flowers, produce, meats and breads.

Andra is our guide. A local Latvian in her 30s, she is old enough to remember the former Soviet days. "There were times," she says, "when there were meat or milk shortages. Food was not as abundant as it is now."

But times have changed, and the market is overflowing with produce. "Here are some of our favorite foods," she says, picking up a loaf of black bread, and then pointing out the local mushrooms that Rigans like to hunt for in the forest.

Pickling is a beloved art in Latvia. While many people see little cucumbers, Andra jokes, Latvians see potential pickles. As she talks, I remember the hours that my own mother spent pickling tomatoes, cucumbers and beets from our huge garden. Was this a tiny piece of

Latvian family heritage that had survived through the years?

From the Central Market, we wind our way back into Old Town, passing beautiful cathedrals with Gothic spires, as well as lush green parks, which seem abundant in the city. We stop at the Powder Tower, one of Riga's fortification towers that dates to 1330.

"Your grandpa surely walked past this many times," she says, while I try to imagine his teenage image in the square.

"I'll show you more of his Riga," Andra says, pulling me from my thoughts.

And she does.

We take an elevator to the top of St. Peter's Church, built in 1209. From platforms at the top, we can see a panoramic view of Riga. My eyes scan across the mighty Daugava, and across the red roofs of Old Town. A cruise ship is docked in port, and I can see tiny guests getting off to explore the city.

Then we're off to one of the "hottest" real estate areas in the city – Alberta Street. Riga is known best for its Art Nouveau buildings. This decorative style of architecture was popular in the U.S. and Western Europe from 1890 to WWI. The style uses intricate linear designs and flowing curves to create beautiful buildings that seem like works of art.

In Riga, some of the best Art Nouveau buildings can be found on Alberta Street. Many of them had just been finished in 1915, when my grandpa lost his family. Most of the structures fell into disrepair in the following decades, but have been lovingly restored today. Alberta Street is now home to many embassies and international companies.

Riga, especially Old Town, is tidy and attractive, and it's hard to imagine all that it has been through. But then we pass a small monument behind St. Jacob's Church that was erected after Latvia gained its freedom. Andra translates for us: "God give us the strength and intelligence so that we will never let anyone enslave us again."

Enslave. The word saddens me greatly, and I realize its truth when we reach the Corner Building, also known as the KGB Building.

While the rest of Riga glimmers in restored beauty, the Corner Building is old, run down and ugly. For years, the Latvians have been debating what to do with it. After all, what do you do with a building that you hate, but is still part of your history?

Once a lovely structure built in 1912, the building was commandeered by the Nazis in 1940. From there, the Nazis orchestrated their rule of terror, killing more than 70,000 Latvian Jews without thought, and imprisoning many Latvians for the slightest infractions. But the building's horrible story was just beginning. When the Nazis left, the KGB took over.

As we enter the building, I see a small sign. Translated, it reads: "I believe these times will vanish like a horrible nightmare. It gives me strength to stand here and breathe. Our nation has suffered a lot and has learned to survive and it will survive these dark times too."

Inside, our young tour guide takes us through the building, telling its story in a somber, yet forthright tone. "In most places," she says, "the war ended in 1945. But for Soviet-occupied countries like Latvia, the war didn't end till 1990."

The Soviets controlled everything and everyone. Those who dared to protest – such as one elderly farmer's wife who grumbled when the Soviets took her farm – were thrown into the dank, crowded cells in the bottom floor of the building.

The "cells" are about as large as a walk-in closet, and they were crowded and dirty. The KGB kept the lights on constantly and the heat or cold temperatures at extreme. They wanted to make each prisoner as miserable as they could. Food and water was withheld, torture was common. Many prisoners were simply killed.

Our group is silent, for it is hard to comprehend such cruelty to fellow human beings. I wonder then if my family who was lost that day on the bridge survived only to suffer under the grinding thumb of the Nazis and Soviets. The ache in my heart grows as we walk through the building. As we come up from the lower floors of the prison, our guide talks more about life in Latvia today. As young as she is, she still knows stories of the past. Even in the 1980s, she tells us, the mother of one of her friends was arrested and interrogated by the KGB for singing a funny song about the lack of meat in the country. The woman was only 17 at the time.

The talk eventually turns to Russia today. "It is hard to live next to Russia," our guide says. "We have lost much to that country."

The group is silent as we listen. From what we've seen and heard at the KBG Building, that feeling is understandable.

*****

Having learned about the Latvia of the past, we're ready to explore the vibrant Latvia of today.

Its culture is filled with centuries-old traditions, and singing is one of them. Every five years, Latvia gets together to sing at the Nationwide Song and Dance Celebration. There are contests and parades, where some 30,000 Latvians wearing traditional folk costumes and flowers in their hair fill the streets. The culmination is a gala concert where thousands of Latvians sing and dance together as one.

Determined to see some local music ourselves, we head to a restaurant called *Folkklubs Ala Pagrabs*. Housed in a cellar, it's known for its large selection of local beers, live music and dancing.

Red bricks line the cellar walls, and candles light up several nooks and crannies. The rooms are filled with young Latvians, and we soon learn why.

The food and beer are excellent – and cheap. Ben orders a local caramel beer for 2 euros. It's only 1 euro for the soup of the day. We ask our waitress, a young blonde woman in her early 20s, to bring us whatever local Latvian foods are her favorite.

She starts off with Latvian garlic bread – sticks of black bread baked with chunks of butter and garlic served with herb sour cream sauce. Already I'm in heaven.

Then she brings us Latvian meatballs and sweet red sauerkraut. It's unlike any kraut I've ever had, and it's fantastic.

As we eat, a violinist and accordionist come to the stage. As they start to play a selection of folk music I don't recognize, the young people around us start to jump up. Tables are moved and chairs are cleared.

And then they dance. Not the usual haphazard dancing that fills most American clubs, but authentic and precise folk dances. No one misses a step, and they dance with enthusiasm, laughing as they move.

Ben and I are enthralled. "How do you guys know all these dances?" we ask our waitress.

"Oh we learn them in school," she replies. "That's how we have kept our language and culture through all the different occupations." And then she's off to serve someone else.

She stops by again to serve us dessert of black bread pudding and sliced apples with whipped cream.

"What brings you to Latvia?" she asks.

"Well, I came to learn more about my heritage," I reply. "But next time, I think I'll come back just because I want to be in Latvia."

*****

There are some moments that you know to enjoy and savor as they happen – and this is one of them. As we walk back from the restaurant to our hotel, I listen to the sound of our footsteps on the cobblestone, and concentrate on the soft sounds of Latvian around me. It is like no other language I've heard, and I've tried over the last few days to learn a few words. After all, I know I will be back.

But as we walk through the hotel courtyard with its hanging flowers and happy-sounding fountain to our room, I think of one very important word that I haven't learned yet.

"I'll be right back," I tell Ben, and rush back to the front desk. The woman working there tonight kindly obliges my request for a one-word Latvian language lesson.

"The word is *vectēvs*," she says with a smile.

I try to say it, but the word is awkward on my tongue, heavy with lost years and family history.

"It's OK," she smiles. "Try again."

"*Vectēvs*," I say again, picturing the man whose legacy I have felt here in Riga.

It is the Latvian word for grandfather.

Janna Graber is an American travel journalist, editor and producer who has covered travel in more than 38 countries. She fell in love with exploring other countries and cultures while studying abroad in Austria, and has been hooked ever since. She is the managing editor at GoWorldTravel.com, and has written for Parade, Reader's Digest, Outside, Chicago Tribune and many more. Read more of her work at jannagraber.com or follow her on Twitter @AColoradoGirl.

ASIA NICHOLS

MONKEY WRENCH
Indonesia

Forget surfing, forget shameless beach sex, and forget trekking to Komodo Island to see Indonesia's man-eating dragons. All my plans for a tropical adventure are officially dead.

"Dammit guy!" I cry out. "It hurts. It hurts. It really hurts!"

"Sorry," says Russ. That's my husband.

You want to hear what adventure looks like from where I'm sitting? Let me tell you: It looks like a crappy $7-a-night bungalow with sweaty ceilings, a springy mattress, an itchy mosquito net and a family of gigantic cockroaches playing freeze tag in the mildewy bathroom.

I breathe out, gripping the edge of the bed. "All right! I'm all right."

With caution, Russ lifts the rest of me onto the mattress and props my banged-up leg on top of a backpack and two pillows. He flicks on the fan but no air blows. Power is out again — fantastic! That means for the next several hours I not only have half the use of my legs, but now I'm easy prey for the vermin. Helluva way to start life in Lombok, eh? Restless, I tear open a pack a garlic peanut puffs and pop two in my mouth.

After living in Chiang Mai, Thailand, for the past three months, I came here ready for the natural world — ready to explore fishing villages, add some Bahasa Indonesia to my vocabulary, leap off cliffs into the sea, you know, like the adventurous types. Unfortunately, life had other plans. So what happened? I'll tell you what happened. It all started one week ago, when I first learned of a place called Monkey Forest.

*****

Our Air Asia flight from Bangkok arrived at the international airport in Surabaya after 11:45 p.m. A half-hour later, our taxi driver pulled up to a shadowy hostel covered in moss and vines. The place looked like an abandoned refuge. The kind of place you'd throw rocks at as a kid then run like hell.

After six attempts at the doorbell, a tiny light shone through the window. A grinning woman opened the door. She was stout with full cheeks, curly short hair and a long, white buttonless nightgown. She spoke very hushed and called herself Dhyana, the hostel owner. Dhyana ushered us up a winding flight of white tile stairs and into a cell-like room furnished with twin beds.

Next day, we awoke to the early-morning adhān, the Islamic call to prayer, trumpeting over loudspeakers. Afterward, Dhyana made breakfast. Light rain turned into a thunderstorm. Russ and I stayed inside all day. That night, I couldn't sleep through the rumble so while Russ was out cold upstairs, I joined Dhyana in the main room. And that's when she told me the story of Monkey Mountain.

Monkey Mountain is a dark folktale that terrified Dhyana when she was young. It is a secret place in the forest where mothers and fathers go to ask the devil for riches. The devil delights in the begging parents and finally promises to grant their desires. But they return home to find that, in exchange for riches, the soul of their child is gone, forever trapped inside the forest monkeys.

I sat crossed-legged, wide-eyed like a kid, entranced. Dhyana stared at me with the strangest look on her face, as if I had to be some kind of twisted nut to enjoy such a story. Thing is, I always had a funny fixation with tales that have unpleasant endings.

One week later, when our ferry docked at Lombok and I learned there was a place on the island called Monkey Forest, I told Russ we had to check it out. Usually, my husband has no interest in wildlife. He's just not one of those characters. And so, to get my wish, I promised him that on the way back from the forest, we could stop at a secluded beach where I would make the trip worth his while.

*****

The next morning, we rented a motorbike.

"Uh, you sure you feel comfortable on this thing?" I asked Russ, clutching his waist.

"Yeah," he said, revving the motorbike.

That would be the sixth time I asked. Russ was ready to make good of my promise, and nags about safety were killing his mood. But this was our first time driving abroad and Americans don't drive on the left side of the road. Of all the accidents foreigners face, I had heard motorbikes are the deadliest and most common. So naturally, I was unnerved.

But then I had to catch myself because law of attraction says what we think is what we manifest. So I replaced thoughts of crashing and blood spatter with thoughts of cute little monkeys and picking out a sandy love nest. I gave our helmets a final tug and gripped Russ tight as the bike sputtered smoke then whipped into the road, headed for Monkey Forest.

*****

I kept getting smacked in the face by great winds as we rode the hilly terrain. But I didn't mind. We had nothing but sunny skies and pretty green mountains ahead of us. It was a quiet drive, a weekday, so the road was empty except for a few lone vehicles. I looked to my left. I could see the coastline with its fresh cerulean waters. I spotted a slew of perahus anchored ashore and fishers reclined against shady nut trees.

"Am I holding too tight?" I said, nose mushed into my husband's back.

"Nope," said Russ, cruising the steep slope.

Before long, the fuel gauge crept down to empty. I kept watch for petrol dealers — gasoline is called "petrol" out here. Petrol looks like urine in glass bottles sold on the side of the road. We stopped at a fishing village and while a dealer put petrol into the tank, I bought a cold bottled drink from the snack stand and asked the locals how much farther was Monkey Forest. Fingers pointed up the road. Most spoke Bahasa, but there were a few who studied English. That's how I found out about snacks.

"It is not nice to see monkeys without snacks," said the petrol dealer.

"If you have snacks, everything will be fine," said the snack stand owner.

"I like the beach. I do not go up there," said a 50-year-old fisher in an Orlando Magic jersey. "But with snacks, you will be OK."

So we got snacks. Back on the bike, we rode a few more kilometers up the road.

"How about here?" I said, pointing to a snack cart.

Russ eased on the throttle. I scanned the cluttered cart and pointed. The cart owner ripped off 10 small packs of garlic peanut puffs and handed them to me.

"*Terima kasih*," I said, passing him a blue-purple bill.

"Want any?" I called back to Russ.

"Are those for humans?" Russ asked, thinking it over from the bike.

I flipped over the pack, but the labels read in Bahasa. I brought the pack to my nose and sniffed. Smelled like garlic to me.

"I don't know, I can't tell."

"I'm good," he said.

I signaled to the cart owner and held up the peanut puffs. "Monkeys?"

He pointed up the road. I shrugged and tossed the snacks into my bag. I hopped back on the bike, giddy-like, because 3 kilometers away was the fabled forest.

*****

I spotted a monkey sitting on a wooden post.

"Over there Russ. Slow down — look," I said, clenching my bag. "Pull over."

As my eyes adjusted to the dim light of the dark forest, monkeys with long tails and pointed heads started popping up everywhere. Some scampered across the road. Others huddled near the trees or swung from branches. Russ slowed down and found a clear space on the side of the narrow road on the hill. He pulled over and turned off the bike. I hung my helmet, looking around in awe.

A few monkeys scooted toward us. Careful not to move too suddenly, I snuck a pack of peanut puffs to Russ.

"So I guess we just feed them," I said, reaching for the camera.

Russ threw a peanut puff. Monkeys leaped from their posts. He threw another. I watched as my hand fished for my camera, somewhere in my bag. A gang of monkeys started moving our way. Five, 10, hundreds, I'm guessing. Within seconds, their numbers tripled. My anxious hand fumbled over a glasses case, packs of peanut puffs, a cosmetics bag. Where the hell was this camera? Fumbling, fumbling. More fumbling.

Monkeys were getting closer. To distract them, Russ heaved the whole bag. Dozens of tiny white puffs rolled across the skinny, dirt road. Monkeys raced after the skittering snacks. But the clever ones were not fooled and headed straight for the source.

Panicked, I glanced down to grab more snacks and, to my horror, saw that two of the rascals had come within inches of my ankle. Suddenly, I was 10 years old again.

*****

It was my birthday. I was having a pool party at my nana's house. The backyard was ringing with sounds of laughter and splashing water. Mommy set a pretty cake in the center of a picnic table next to a stack of shiny boxed gifts and money envelopes. Smoke oozed from the old-fashioned pit while daddy flipped ribs and slathered them in sweet sauce. A call to sing to Happy Birthday sent a rush of little legs clamoring out of the pool to sit around the cake. I took a great big breath and blew out 10 candles. Kids sat in chairs and on steps eating cake and ice cream when suddenly we heard a loud scream.

Someone spotted a fat hairy possum. Cakes flew, guests scattered, running in every direction. Daddy dashed around with his water hose and cigarette, trying to nail the fat sucker. Kids in colorful swimsuits stood shivering on chairs. Horrified, I found a spot in the corner and stayed there, trembling, wishing things would just go back to normal.

I glanced down at my feet...and there it was, frozen stiff, its thin possum mouth curved into a grotesque grin, showing its disgusting pink gums and razor sharp choppers. The thing was soaked and shivering like the kids, hiding from daddy and his hose. I hollered.

*****

"Russ, go!" I said, snapping back to the present. I tossed my leg over the bike. Forget snacks, forget taking pictures. I just wanted to get out of that crazy forest!

Russ started the motor. More monkeys rushed over. The two rascals were eyeballing my ankle, preparing for the tear.

"Go! Go! Get me the hell out of here!" I shrieked, grasping my husband's shoulder.

And the bike zoomed away. Without me.

*****

I never knew I could fly before then. And I was soaring. But the funny thing about flying is you don't really know you're flying — until you fall. For a beat, I felt my left leg stretch long and far, trying to hold onto a bike that's moving in full gear. Then the bike disappeared. The sunlight disappeared. The trees disappeared, too. I felt warm all over. My eyes fluttered and I felt like drifting to sleep...

"Asia! Hey, Asia! You OK?" Russ had his hands on my back, sitting me up.

"I don't think I landed right," I heard myself mutter.

I took a moment to orient myself, then looked around. My legs were sprawled out on the gravel. No bones poking out. No blood. But I hurt really bad and an Indonesian man with a blurry face was rubbing my feet.

"OK?" asked Blurry Face.

My eyes flapped open and shut. Sweat gushed down my face. Hands pressed against my foot, wiggled my toes, and squeezed my legs for tender spots. I tried to stand.

"Watch it," said Russ. "You're moving too fast."

I felt breakfast bitching in my belly. I leaned forward, parted my legs, ready to spit up nasi goreng. I gagged and spat. Nothing else came out. A few feet away, I glimpsed a monkey gnawing on my favorite sandal. Nearby, more grim-looking monkeys were watching. The Indonesian man hissed at them. Some scrammed. Russ helped me stagger to my bare feet. I frowned at the mechanical deathtrap, parked off the road.

"Do you want to go to the hospital?" Russ asked.

"No," I said. "Just let me rest."

Four hands hoisted me onto the leather seat. With my legs and feet safely secured, I thanked Blurry Face for stopping to help. He got onto his motorbike and waited for us to go.

"You good?" Russ asked, looking back at me.

I nodded.

"You sure you're good?" he said, gripping the bike handles.

I nodded again and tightened my arms around his waist. Slower than ever, he eased back onto the road and let the wheels start rolling. My head sunk into Russ' back and I tried hard as I could not to close my eyes.

You know, my mind tends to make these strange connections. Like why things happen the way they do. I thought about why this accident happened on the ride back. Was I not supposed to come to Monkey Forest? Were we supposed to fly into the Philippines instead of Indonesia like we talked about? Or am I too cowardly to be the adventurous type? I never figured it out. And when I raised my eyes, the sun had fallen and we were pulling up to our bungalow.

*****

So you wanted to know how it happened. Well, there you have it. I'm on one-month respite with a sweaty wrap on my banged-up left leg and just two packs of peanut puffs to go before I'm out. The door creaks open. In walks Russ, coming to check on me again. He flicks on the fan. It rattles and spins. Russ' hand brushes my toes. He gives me a suggestive look.

I try to imagine myself with my husband on one of those deserted beaches, thanking him thoroughly for accommodating me. I imagine us going surfing in those cerulean waters and trekking to see the Komodo dragons. OK, maybe not the dragons. Dragons look like monkeys. And possums. But none of that matters now that I'm here on one of the world's most stunning islands, bedridden on a springy mattress in a vermin-infested bungalow. Bye-bye tropical adventures.

Russ takes the peanut puffs from my pathetic hand.

"Hey!" I pout.

He ignores me. Then he moves close, reaches down, and scoots the backpack from under my bruised leg to give him space.

"I was eating those," I said, glancing at that half-full bag of puffs. "They taste good, you know."

In 2011, Asia Nichols left her home in northern California to backpack with her husband across Southeast Asia, India and Nepal. Fascinated by local folklore, this two-year adventure inspired her to write stories. Her nonfiction works have appeared in publications including Ebony, The New York Times and Whole Life Times Magazine.

TODD PITOCK

LETTERS FROM THE COUNTRYSIDE
Czech Republic

I had come to the countryside to get out of Prague. The Czech capital is enchanting, a colorful bricolage of buildings — yet perhaps even too charming, attracting herds of tourists who heave down from Hradcany, the castle on the city's highest hill, across the Charles Bridge and into Old Town Square. It threatens to turn the city into not only a canned experience but an effacing one.

I wanted to get deeper inside the place, away from the noise of pubs, to where I could hear stories. Now was a good time, too. A quarter-century since the Velvet Revolution began a period of democracy and relative prosperity, some people were digging into a past that had been buried under layers and debris of 20th century calamities — falling empires, rising nationalism, Nazis and

Communists. It made people reflect on the strange turns of their lives.

"My father was a high official with the Communists," Zdenka Noskova told me. "After the revolution, everyone was outside singing and dancing and celebrating, and he was inside his room with the shades pulled down. He didn't want to watch. But he also went straight to the phone and began calling people he knew. He was making business. It was like that with all the Communists. They lost the government power, but they had the contacts. The people who celebrated were still poor after and the people who were sad got all the money."

"So he became a capitalist?"

"No. He still says he is a Communist — a Communist businessman."

I decided I would go by bicycle, and set out on the trails and secondary roads that vein the countryside.

*****

On the way south, not all that far from Prague, I met Antonin Dvorak. I was in Nelahozeves, his ancestral home.

He was a sturdy 80-year-old and carried in one arm a timid and tiny Yorkie named Haffi who was about his age in dog years. He took me to the estate where his grandfather, the great composer, wrote many of his major works. He used a heavy metal key to open a big wooden door of a stone wall surrounding the property and we walked up a path toward a house within a sprawling forest of spindly trees.

A second-floor room had a dining table and a puffed-up feather bed in a corner that made it feel as if it had all just been tidied up before whoever lived there returned home. On the walls were framed letters and sepia photographs of Dvorak, and when my Dvorak stood next to them, you could see that the patriarch had left the world his music but left his grandson his face, his deep-set eyes under the eaves of heavy brows, a wide nose and swept-back gray hair.

The family tradition was always to name one son Antonin. It must have been part honor and part affliction to be labeled a facsimile at birth, because, of course, there could be only one "real" Dvorak.

But my Dvorak seemed happy to bask in his grandfather's reflected glory — though it had shined relatively late in life.

"Before the Velvet Revolution," he said, dropping his chin between rising shoulders, "I was only Dvorak." He worked as an engineer in a nuclear energy plant and though he was clearly an intelligent man, he'd been a cog in the industrial wheel of the Soviet satellite. "But after the Velvet Revolution," he said, waving his hand boldly as if he were conducting a symphony, "I was Dvorak!"

There were different reasons that seem absurd looking back, and were probably just as absurd at the time, that had to do with Czech nationalism and the Communists, and their questions about Dvorak's patriotism due, insanely, to time Dvorak spent in Spillville, Iowa. In any case, this Dvorak's story was unusual only in that his grandfather was so famous. In another way, though, it was emblematic how 1989 had been like the parting of the Red Sea, of black and white before, versus an immensely bright and colorful after.

*****

A couple of days later I rolled into Klatovec, a tiny village in the Czech Highlands. On a narrow road lit up by wild red poppies and purple lupines, I turned off into the woods and arrived at a forge.

They were a family of blacksmiths. Alfred "Freddie" Habermann, 60, greeted me with his sons Josef and David. They were ready to get down to business.

"OK, you're here, so let's do some smithing," Josef said. He and David, wearing leather aprons and bandanas, fired up the furnace. They held a metal rod with tongs in the furnace until its blackness turned orange-red and became like taffy, and then they began pounding it, the two of them together, creating a shrill, rhythmic banging.

"Blacksmith music," said Freddie, with a discernible twinkle in his eyes.

Blacksmiths had thrived for generations in the Czech Republic. The ubiquitous countryside castles needed enough work that a diligent, skilled smith could bang out a good living, and its location as a central European crossroad meant that people were constantly bringing in new knowledge, materials and techniques. The Communists quashed all of that. Aesthetic endeavors were considered bourgeois; there were no more commissions from castles, remnants of a decadent past now left to decay. It was all factory work, and how many hammers and sickles could a smith do? The Iron Curtain closed off the flow of people and knowledge.

For people like Freddie's father, Alfred, it became as if they'd cut the supply of oxygen. A renowned master known as "the pope of the blacksmiths," he got permission to emigrate in 1985. Freddie was barred from working until the Velvet Revolution put him back in business. Eventually Josef and David apprenticed with him; another son makes horseshoes while a daughter is a goldsmith and jewelry designer. Alfred died in 2008 at age 84.

"Freedom is everything to a blacksmith," said Freddie.

Josef and David finished pounding and shaping the piece they worked on — a Habermann leaf, which is their signature — and now they put it aside so we could tour the property as it cooled and hardened.

Each Habermann had a specialty, and as they walked me through the forge and the garden outside I got to see some samples of their work. Freddie, known for his gates, does abstract works, such as one featuring two attenuated shafts of metal, one bending toward the other, which he named "Resolution." Another was a large mobile of oval shafts that he called "The Universe." A devout Catholic, his work also contained religious motifs.

Josef's specialty was restoration. He showed me a lockbox whose labyrinthine mechanism he'd reconstructed through reverse-engineering. Restoration also seemed symbolic of the blacksmiths, and the family.

I thanked them for taking time to show me around.

"Wait," Josef said. He disappeared into the forge and came out holding the Habermann leaf. "Here," he said, handing it to me. "We made it for you."

It was a lovely gift, though as I continued biking, I realized that they'd already given me a better one: new eyes on the castles, which suddenly became visible to me for their gates and grills, lamps and locks, all the ways the blacksmiths put their marks on them.

If there was a sense that they had triumphed, I wanted to see the thing they had triumphed over. Under a thick cover of clouds, I pedaled until I arrived in Cizov (chee-sof), a tiny Czech village in southern Bohemia along the border with Austria. The main attraction was the Czech Republic's last remnant of the Iron Curtain.

Its small stone houses were set close to one another, and I felt the bicycle juddering on the rutted main road. I didn't see anything resembling a storefront, but found a tavern where a merry troupe of spandex-clad cyclists quaffed golden pilsners around a long picnic table. It was 9 a.m. The ones who spoke no English at all laughed at the ones who tried, insisting that I join in their liquid whole grain breakfast.

German-speaking people had populated the region for most of the five centuries it was part of the Austro-Hungarian Empire. Czechs and Slovaks united as a country in 1923. In 1938, the Nazis invaded and annexed the region they called the Sudetenland, and when the Allies liberated it in 1945, the Czech government expelled 3.5 million German speakers whom they perceived as Nazi sympathizers and collaborators. Needing to re-populate the region to sustain industry and agriculture, they offered incentives for Czechs from other parts of the country to move in.

Then, as Churchill later popularized the phrase, an Iron Curtain descended across the continent, and Cizov became an Eastern Bloc frontier town, a militarized zone to watch the Austrian border and keep its own people from fleeing across it — until 1989, when the historical tremors settled, and the world came back into focus.

I rode up a path. On one side a light wind combed a field of yellow-brown wheat. On the other was the barbed wire fence, which ran for several hundred meters to a squat and gloomy black watchtower. It was the original, and yet looked like a strange piece of protest art. I thought of a Czech man I'd spoken to in upstate New York, another blacksmith named Vaclav Barina, who in the 1980s escaped by clawing his way under the fence — a feat of desperation that was even harder to imagine seeing the physical layout.

A young couple rode up, got off their bikes and pulled out a camera. The man climbed up the watchtower's metal stairs and the woman ordered him to come down. They put their cheeks together and he held his camera with a straight arm to record the moment. I offered to take their picture.

"Make the tower be in the picture," he said. He learned English working a chair lift in Vermont for two seasons.

I asked if the place had any particular memory or meaning to him.

"It was a horrible period," he said. "Thank God it's over. I was just a kid so it didn't affect me, but my father tells stories. He patrolled in Germany, but it was all like this. He had to serve two years with the army. Once, he took off his uniform jacket because it was too hot, and he was walking with it under his arm like this, and the other soldiers started shooting at him." He pantomimed someone using a machine gun.

"Why did they shoot?"

"They thought he was trying to escape."

His father had come here two years ago, revisiting a time many would just as soon forget, probably the way someone fingers a scar left by a bad accident. He arrived, looked at the fence, and left.

I took their photograph and handed over my camera so they could take mine, too. Then we climbed on our bikes, said so-long, and put the Cold War behind us.

*****

Many villages and towns brimmed with charm. Perched on mountains, their sloping roofs capped brightly-painted homes, and narrow lanes led to cobblestone squares with clock towers and church spires. Often, castles were perched high above. (People often assume the Prague Castle, or Hradcany, was Kafka's model, but the novel isn't set in Prague, and any of these towns could be the setting.) Between these hamlets were great fields of barley, meadows speckled with wild red poppies, horse paddocks, and forests framing cultivated fields of sunflowers.

There were lost souls, people consciously reenacting the past, and deep souls endeavoring to plumb it.

East of Cizov, I arrived in Mikulov, just north of the Austrian border, and checked into the Hotel Templ — the name referred to its prior use as a synagogue — and took a walk up what for centuries had been the Jews' street. Some of the disused temples and study houses were re-purposed, some rehabilitated. The addresses on Jewish homes had once been marked with Latin numerals to differentiate them from Christian homes that used Arabic numerals.

As a Jew, I couldn't help but be fascinated by the Jewish history of Czechoslovakia. The 600-year-old community produced a census of major figures, rabbis and writers, mystics and merchants. In the 20th century they had become cosmopolitan and acculturated in ways that I found very relatable. (Kafka, who had a kind of religious and Zionist awakening toward the end of his life, criticized his father, a shop owner, for going to synagogue only on high holidays.) The community had grown to 375,000 people before the Nazis annihilated them, and then the Communists did their best to blot out their memory by barring serious discussion of them. Even now, though, they occupied a place in the consciousness of many Czechs, and one of Prague's must-see spots is the Jewish cemetery in the Josevov neighborhood. What better place to encounter a dead community?

Mikulov's Jewish cemetery bore certain similarities; the big difference was that no one else was there. Just to get in required finding someone with a key, and then, once inside it was a haunting place. It contained thousands of graves. Over six centuries the dead had outgrown the space. Headstones were uprooted and stacked sideways to create a retaining wall to build the cemetery up and make more burial space. Jewish DNA here ran deep, quite literally. Religious Jews come to visit graves of *tzadakim*, or holy men, lighting candles and leaving behind personal prayers and messages in pieces of paper, which was scattered like litter.

And yet it was a sign of life. Some headstones were so old that it was hard to make out their heavily eroded Hebrew letters. Trees grew all over the place at strange angles, sometimes twisting and misshapen, even out of the graves themselves, pushing the steles sideways. No

Jews lived or were buried in Mikulov since the 1940s — a few Holocaust survivors had returned briefly after World War II but did not stay. Authorities, who did not permit any acknowledgment of Jews, barred anyone from entering the graveyard. Left to themselves, trees had self-seeded and grown wildly. When people entered the cemetery in the 1990s, a controversy arose between those who wanted to clean it up and those who saw the haunted forest as a part of the historical record they wanted to preserve.

So far, the trees had stayed, and the focus was rather on unearthing the memory of the community, which had once been in the thick of things when Mikulov was the region's hub. At its peak, the population grew to 35,000. One of the most famous figures is not buried here. Rabbi Judah Loew is the 16th-century sage known for promulgating the myth of the Golem, the forerunner of Frankenstein, though the Jewish version, a Kabbalistic fable, has a more mystical underpinning. He was chief rabbi here before he went to Prague.

The rich history was obliterated, and after the destruction it was obscured. The tragic ending, though, also obscured the fact that life here had once been good. One person who had plumbed the past and literally mined the earth that contained it was a local painter, Sylva Chludilova. I went to see her on the old Jewish street, where her building, once a cheder, a Jewish study house, contained her gallery and living quarters.

Sylva was a matronly woman who wore a loose-fitting dress and, at 47, carried herself in a way that suggested she'd given up all vanity. We sat under the vaulted ceiling of her garden-level apartment, and, as twilight shadows dimmed the room, we progressed from tea to shots of *medovina*, a local honey wine.

"Do you like it?" she asked.

She was delighted to hear that I did.

Sylva didn't remember any particular event that spurred her interest. Like the trees in the cemetery, her interest in the Jews had just seeded itself.

"When I read the stories or see these things," she said, referring to Jewish objects such as ritual candelabras and scrolls, "I just felt something. In school, you couldn't talk about anything Jewish. The Holocaust was never mentioned. You couldn't talk about it openly, in case it made someone suspicious."

"Do you have any Jewish roots?" I asked.

"Maybe. We don't know."

The Jews had deep roots in Mikulov, but it had suffered grievous blows from which it could not recover. Even after the Nazis, some Jewish survivors returned to find that for one reason for another — often someone had made themselves comfortable in their homes or weren't eager to return things given for safekeeping — they were no longer welcome. They had left, and now Sylva was the closest there was to a Jewish presence.

Her work hung from the walls, and canvasses of various sizes were stacked or set upright in clusters against the wall. Her style included layering light with shades of white, gray and black. Portraits of holy men and other imagery drew on the Hebrew alphabet. Some works alluded to Jewish legends, such as one about a rabbi who buried a menorah during a pogrom, though only he knew where it was. Centuries later another rabbi who knew it existed prayed until he saw seven stars pointing to it.

She related to the story in particular because from the time she first moved to the apartment, she'd found signs of Jewish life in her garden, like signs to the past. And like the cemetery up the street, it included both what was buried and what grew on its own.

"How so?" I asked.

"I go outside and dig," she said. "I find buttons, pieces of ceramic, a prayer book."

"How often do you find something?" I asked.

She smiled coyly. "Every time," she said.

*****

In Telč, a town about two hours from Prague in the Czech Highlands, rain beat down like a parade of drums. I met Zdenka Noskova, the woman whose father became the Communist businessman. We'd been introduced by a mutual acquaintance who told me about a memorial Zdenka created, and she'd offered to take me there.

At 37, Zdenka had a demure manner. She wore her auburn hair short, and dressed in a long skirt. She worked in a print shop, though the lasting imprint she'd made had been a walking trail, and later, a memorial she'd created to the memory of a Jewish painter who died in the Holocaust.

We drove out of town in a downpour until we arrived in her village, Kostelni Myslove, a pastoral scene of meadows divided by stacked stone borders, and old houses with dark, slanted roofs. We got out of the car and took shelter from the rain at a bus stop.

Just after they married, Zdenka's husband brought her to Kostelni, whose population consisted of 50 mostly old people. Boredom and isolation made Zdenka swoon into depression, and she'd sit for hours by a window looking out onto a crumbling old farmhouse at one end of the one-street village.

One day she began investigating the ruin. It had belonged to a man named Frantisek Nagl, who inherited the land and lived there with his wife and two children. He had no enthusiasm for farming. He loved to paint.

The neighbors regarded him as different. But it was not only because he was an artist. It was also because the Nagls were Kostelni's only Jews. After the German invasion, the Nazis found them and put them on a transport to Terezin, the concentration camp near Prague, and then to Auschwitz. The whole family perished.

Five years after Terezin was liberated, 250 of Nagl's works, an archive of watercolors and gouaches of the barracks, bunks and courtyards, were found hidden in a wall in the camp.

At first no one welcomed Zdenka's quest. She wondered what secrets they might have that they didn't want to dredge up the past. It was an unfortunate truth in a lot of places that some people profited from the Jewish tragedy, inheriting property whose provenance they didn't want to be reminded of. Even the existing Jewish community in Brno, though, wondered about her motive, and whether she, too, was looking to profit.

But Zdenka had only yearned to know, and then to remember and honor Nagl, who, like her, had had to make the best of things in a place that had been chosen for him. She created the trail. It runs for several hundred yards through a meadow and a patch of forest posted with plaques about Nagl.

"The trail is not the best thing in the world," she said. "It is very simple. But you cannot understand 6 million. You can understand one person."

Eventually people started traveling here to see it.

Zdenka wrote a biography and created a second memorial in 2002, along with Phoenix Telc and Phoenix Berlin, civic associations that preserve Jewish history. By then, the early resistance had faded, and volunteers came to help plant fruit trees to line the road leading up to the memorial — a stone table and benches surrounded by lindens, the Czech national tree. It's at the peak of a hill where clouds hang low over meadows. A curtain of mist falls over a ridge of hills that roll into the distance.

"Nagl loved to paint here," Zdenka said. It was his own Mont Sainte-Victoire.

Then, one day after the memorial had been there a while, vandals marked it with a swastika.

But by then Zdenka had achieved something unlikely: She had revived Nagl in the hearts of her neighbors. She had rendered the artist, made him visible. And now, they came out, many of the same people who had opposed her quest, to scrub the memorial clean.

"It gave me my life back," she told me.

Zdenka had often wondered what Nagl looked like, but the only photograph she had ever found showed only his back as he painted on an easel. After news coverage of the community's response to the vandalism, an envelope arrived out of the blue. It was his picture.

"It is hard to explain how happy it made me," she told me. "After all this time, I finally knew what he looked like."

Todd Pitock writes for various magazines, including National Geographic Traveler, the Atlantic and Discover. He has received awards in the Society of American Travel Writers Foundation Lowell Thomas Travel Journalism Competition and from the American Society of Journalists & Authors. His work has appeared in Best American Science and Nature Writing, Best Travel Writing and Best Jewish Writing.

PETER MANDEL

HIKING THE ANCIENT NAKASENDO WAY
Japan

The moon in Japan is not like our moon. There is no man in there, for one thing. No man, no horn, no cow.

It is nighttime in Kyoto and Shima Enomoto, one of my guides, is pointing up. "Can you see it?" she asks. "Rabbit making a rice cake." She laughs. "Almost a cartoon."

"Maybe it will take some time," I say, looking above rows of buildings, trees with buds about to unwrap, and signs that flash their avenue colors into fire. "Tomorrow we will be on the road," I say. "I'll look again."

It is only day one of my trip, and already life feels strange. It could be jet lag, but the idea of walking fields and mountains and ending up in Tokyo doesn't strike me as realistic. But this is the plan.

The Nakasendo Way tour will guide my group along the route of an ancient and largely forgotten highway. Dating to the 7th century, Japan's Nakasendo was a path for shoguns, pilgrims and samurai — not to mention average travelers like we are — who wore out pair after pair of straw sandals on the rolling terrain.

Studded with Shinto shrines and statues of deities charged with watching over those on the road, the Nakasendo reached the peak of its usefulness and romance during Japan's Edo Period (1603-1868) before steam trains and paved roads changed the pace of travel. This was a stable time for Japan, under Tokugawa rule. Arts like haiku, woodblock printing, bonsai and Kabuki theater flourished in the larger cities.

One of the most exciting parts of the walk for me is the chance to spend some nights at wayside inns known as ryokan or, when simpler, as minshuku. I once helped to compile a book about the world's oldest family firms and these traditional hostels popped up in the research again and again.

Sure enough, after trudging through bamboo forests during our first day on the road, we turn in at Masuya Inn in the village of Sekigahara — a minshuku which, we're told, has been in business for more than eight centuries. Guest rooms at the inn are carved out by sliding panels made of wood and rice paper, and under our not-very-cushiony futons are floors that have been spread with tatami matting. No shoes are allowed inside and there are special plastic slippers for use only in the bathrooms.

Staying here helps us to immerse ourselves in being part of a group. As will be the case on other nights, we dine at the inn, slipping on robes called yukata and curling up tired legs under the knee-high communal table. One by one, we take turns in the Japanese-style bath, lowering ourselves into a cedar-edged tureen of steaming water and wallowing there until road-tight muscles uncoil.

There are nine of us in the tour group, including Naomi Addyman, a British guide who grew up in Japan; Enomoto, a guide-in-training, and Logan Wong, one of four walkers from Singapore, who informs us that he owns the Yankee Candle distributorship there.

"Yankee Candles?" I ask. "In Singapore?"

"Yes, of course," says Wong, who is dressed for hanging out in a food court, not for hiking. "Extremely popular there. Especially the Lemon Verbena."

We're off on the road right after breakfast the next day, taking advantage of a hazy early spring sun. Plum blossoms are just starting to come out (no cherry yet) and there are puffs of mistletoe in some of the trees. The path is grassy and mostly level this close to Kyoto, winding through rice paddies and around modest farms.

Carol Behm, a professor from Canberra, Australia, points out a patch of violets and yellow kumquat flowers, and someone thinks they see a snake. "It's a stick," I say. "No, it's not," says Addyman. "It's a snake. But it's not a dangerous one."

Every now and then the road leads us into tunnels of shade created by cedar and cypress, and at one point we stop at a sign with a picture of an angry-looking predator. Next to it is a small steel cup. "Ring Bell Against Bear," translates Enomoto with a nervous laugh.

Logan Wong gives it a pull and the sound reverberates around — bouncing back from hills up ahead. "Not to worry," says Addyman. "These are Japanese bears. They're very shy." According to Addyman, the sign-makers should be more worried about the wild boar out here.

But as we begin to climb, no one seems concerned about becoming a snack for animals. Our focus is on learning to pick out the three Japanese characters carved into stone and wooden road signs that designate our route. The first symbol looks like a bird built out of bamboo; the second like the prongs of a pitchfork; and the third like Noah's Ark. Or more like half an ark.

"Middle. Mountain. Way," deciphers Addyman. "That's the Nakasendo — literally translated."

Each day of the walk the road seems slightly steeper, and mountains wearing caps of white step up to dominate the view. It may be because we're working harder, but eating is on everyone's mind.

Meals at our inns have been like edible galleries, with a main exhibit (usually a hot pot) and interesting miniplates on the side presenting forest mushrooms, squares of tofu or sashimi.

"Wish there was a convenience store near here," someone complains as we are picking our way around paving stones that were laid to make the path more predictable for tired feet and hooves.

"No hope, no hope," says Wong. "But Naomi says there's a Boss Coffee machine in the next village. Or it might be the one after."

"Only in Japan," adds Tracey Yeh, a banker from Singapore. "It's vending and more vending. You don't want to run out of change even deep in the woods." Yeh pulls out a bag of Calbee potato chips: soy sauce and mayo flavor. "Want some?" she asks. We pool what we've got.

Wong breaks open a box of Pocky-brand snack sticks. "Rum and raisin," he grins. No one has any rice cakes, but one of the guides offers some deep-fried eel bones in a cellophane pack. To clean our palates there are Kit-Kats. Kit-Kats laced with wasabi. We march on.

We reach the top of a pass where everyone takes a break and where our guides point out a poem, a sad one, that's been inscribed in stone. The author was a princess, we're told. Princess Kazunomiya, who traveled the Nakasendo in the mid-1800s when she was forced to leave Kyoto for Edo to become the shogun's wife.

"Why compose it here?" asks Wong. "Well," says Enomoto, "this is about the point where views back to Kyoto are lost."

From now on, travelers would have turned their thoughts to Edo (now Tokyo). I try this, too. It works until we make it to a town called Okute.

Here, there is a kind of shrine. It's not like those we've passed so far: Most have been small and tidy, with well-made torii gates and statues, sometimes of Jizo Bodhisattva, guardian of travelers. This one is massive. Most have had a sacred rope, a shimenawa, strung across the entrance. This one is hung with twisted branches and with leaves.

It is a tree: a giant cedar. So old, at 1,300 years, that it is thought of as a Shinto deity.

The tree is watching, we are sure, as daypacks slide back on shoulders and we return to the path. Other roadside gods observe our progress in the days to follow. They inspect us as we trudge up even steeper slopes. They know what will happen: Since it is only April, we will walk in snow.

Those that care to regard us from their pedestals and temples — maybe approving, maybe grieving just a bit — as we begin to descend. Our tour, and the Nakasendo itself, end in Tokyo.

From the outskirts, we board a train and tick off some miles sitting down. There is a sense of throwing off a load. And, maybe a little, of guilt. Once in the glass-box city center, we exchange our path for crosswalks. We trace the last few miles on foot.

Our goal, as modern pilgrims, is Tokyo's Nihonbashi Bridge. And almost without realizing it, we are there.

It doesn't look like a woodblock print. It looks like a bridge. Above it is a highway humming with cars. But the cherries are out here. Blossoms spin and fly like confetti when the wind kicks up. Sidewalks, even gutters, look celebratory. Corners of buildings collect drifts of petals. Cars are dusted white, or pink.

Out come cameras and, from the bottom of someone's pack, a single package of Pocky that we somehow missed.

"Have we done it?" asks Tracey Yeh.

"We have," confirms Addyman.

*****

Later that evening, to try and remember it, I make it back to the bridge. I find myself standing underneath a cherry that's only footsteps from where the Nakasendo ends. Its canopy is not like the cedar's. Much more delicate. More frail. Like straw for sandals.

Through branches, I see a streetlight. No, it's rounder, whiter than that: It is the moon.

I think of Shima Enomoto. But she has gone.

"Can you see it?" she would ask. I would not want to tell her. Eleven days from Kyoto, I have looked again. And what I find in the downtown Tokyo moon is not a rabbit. It is not a ricecake.

It is a line through lunar plains and mountains. A path that may have snow, or paving stones, or shrines, for all I know.

The moon of Japan shows a road.

Peter Mandel is an author of books for children including the new "Zoo Ah-Choooo" (Holiday House), "Jackhammer Sam" (Macmillan) and "Bun, Onion, Burger" (Simon & Schuster). A regular travel contributor to The Washington Post and The Boston Globe, he has written for Harper's, The Wall Street Journal, International Herald Tribune and Los Angeles Times. His articles have won several Lowell Thomas awards from the Society of American Travel Writers. He lives in Providence, RI. See petermandel.net

KIMBERLEY LOVATO

FEELING TANZANIA
Tanzania

When I first landed on the scraped dirt airstrip in the Serengeti, giraffes plucked leaves off the canopies of Acacia trees that bordered the runway. A baboon troupe skittered across the road as the single-engine plane came to a halt near an unpainted cement block structure that was the airport. The scene looked made up.

The animals weren't really that close were they? I didn't dare reach out my hand to find out. Was that really an ostrich sprinting across the yellow plains? Did a lion just look me in the eye? This wasn't a zoo or a green-screen backdrop. I was gobsmacked to see zebras and wildebeests and gazelles and warthogs and hippos all loitering within mere feet of one another, and me.

I was later reminded just how real this feral wilderness was when I watched a leopard drag its kill up into a tree and dangle the lifeless, limp-limbed carcass of some antlered animal over a branch. The leopard gnawed and ripped at the decaying flesh for days while trucks of tourists snapped photos from a few meters away.

Africa burrows into your system and it doesn't go away. I'd heard this before. It's a deep, concentrated amalgam of love and longing; of heartache and wonder. Yes, I'd heard this about Africa.

In the early 2000s I was living in Florida and I met a young student from South Africa who'd come to work for a local family as an au pair. Her name escapes me now, but what I do remember about her is that she was homesick for "her continent."

"I miss the rains. I miss the sky. I miss my people and my continent," she'd say when we'd meet at the playground.

Sometimes she'd cry.

It struck me as odd to miss a whole continent. I am a Californian who has moved around a lot, so I missed my friends, my state, and maybe even my city at times. But all of North America? I couldn't relate. I shrugged and patted her on the back, and assumed someday I'd understand.

Someday arrived 15 years later when my family and I went to Tanzania.

The trip was a generous gift from my husband's company, a "thank you" for his 23 years of employment. We opted to go with a company called &Beyond, not only because of its stellar locations around Tanzania, where we planned to focus, and its flawless reputation, but also because of its commitment to conservation and support of local rural villages, which remain in desperate need of attention.

In the Serengeti, we slept in tents. Thick canvas structures I could stand up in, with beds and an "Out of Africa" vibe (sans Robert Redford), but we were not immune to the stagnant midday heat or the biting insects. We took bucket showers outside, the mosquitoes nipping at our ankles and the heated water lugged more than 1,000 feet to us each evening by a skinny boy named Simon who never arrived without a smile and a friendly "*Jambo*."

Melau, our game guide for three days in the Serengeti, is Maasai, he told us, a Nilotic ethnic group of seminomadic people inhabiting southern Kenya and northern Tanzania. We'd later visit a Maasai village, called a *boma*, and step into one of the dirt floor huts barely bigger than a garden shed, with walls and ceilings made of sticks, dirt and cow dung. A rock fire pit was both the home's source of heat and the stove.

"Doesn't it get smoky in here?" my 16-year-old daughter asked.

We were seated on one of two wooden bed platforms that occupied half the space.

"It keeps the mosquitoes away," the Maasai man responded.

The *bomas* are surrounded by thorny trees to keep the lions from attacking the cattle, the lifeblood of the Maasai people. The cows live in the center of the *boma*, inside another circular enclosure, and are tended to by the males of the tribe.

The villagers invited us to dance and jump alongside them while they sang in their native language. We laughed. They laughed with us, or maybe at us, but it didn't matter. Their enthusiasm married us for a few minutes. I admired their sincere smiles and bright clothing, and I hoped the look on my face and my questions reflected a genuine curiosity rather than judgment of their unadorned way of life. I was unable to ripple my body in the fluid way these women could that moved the giant disc necklace up and down on their shoulders. I was too stiff, or too inhibited. Before we left, we bought a few hand-beaded bracelets to bring home to family; the money, we were told, would go to their school and would be used to buy cornmeal for the *boma*.

As Melau drove us around the Serengeti, he rattled off exhaustive knowledge of animals and their behaviors, their habits and their movements. He mimicked the hippo's grumpy-old-man, get-off-my-lawn grunt as the huge mammals wallowed in the river outside our windows, and pointed out the flapping and prancing mating ritual of the ostrich couple we passed each morning. As fascinating to me as these facts were, it was the tales of his childhood that engrossed me.

Chasing lions, being chased by buffalo, trapping guinea fowl so he could sell them for the equivalent of 25 cents — the usual kid stuff for a Maasai kid in Africa, he said. A little different than my upbringing in Los Angeles where I had my own carpeted room and a record player spinning the latest disco albums; where I chased boys and popularity; and where I sold plastic cups of lemonade on the curb for the same price as Melau's guinea fowl.

"You've never slaughtered a chicken?" he asked me. He was sincerely dumbfounded when I shook my head.

"No. No I never have."

The Serengeti girl in me felt somehow deprived of this life skill. I suppressed the city girl privilege that pictured my chicken wrapped neatly in cellophane at my well-stocked, neighborhood grocery store. The first time I ever saw a whole, dead chicken was as a young woman at a market in France. It hung by its pale feet, eyes glazed, its partially opened beak evermore gasping its last breath. Its skin was plucked bare, save for the few downy stragglers that shimmied in the breeze. I stared at it for a few minutes wondering what on earth I'd ever do with a whole, dead chicken. Of course I knew where my sanitized grocery store version came from but, like most, I preferred not to think about meat's earthly forms.

Every now and then Melau would stop the vehicle, turn the engine off and listen. Like a tuning fork to the wild he'd grab binoculars and scan 180 degrees along the hazy heat line where the grass seeped into the sky. Sometimes he'd see something, the flick of a tail or the twitch of an ear, or an interloping bright color in the drape of uniformed neutrality that was the Serengeti landscape. Another time he stopped to observe a herd of gazelle and declared, "They don't look relaxed."

I hadn't noticed, but now that he mentioned it — what were they worried about? My eyes darted around the plains like an unsettled beast, and I watched for something. Or was something watching me? I suddenly felt like the hunted.

Later he stopped the truck, slammed it into reverse, and slowly rewound our trajectory while sniffing the air until he found the precise spot.

"Smell that?"

"What?"

He inhaled the warm and dusty wind into his flared nostrils.

"That. It's the smell of broken Acacia tree. There are elephants near."

A pungent whiff of an unfamiliar African incense drifted up my nose. It was green and wet and musky. Melau was right, there was an elephant nearby. Once we found it, we watched it break branches for 15 minutes before it got bored with us and disappeared deeper into the African thicket.

We left the Serengeti and took a bush plane to Lake Manyara, a lush and verdant national park and lake, home to more than 1 million flamingoes that, from a distance, looked like a ribbon of rose petals scattered atop a glassy bath.

I visited the village of Mayorka to see firsthand the community work that &Beyond was doing. I'd heard the company had built a couple of primary school buildings and a medical facility. As we walked the village's dirt road lined with cornfields with our young 20-year-old local guide Salu, barefoot children with brilliant teeth and ill-fitted clothing ran to us and waved. "*Jambo! Jambo!*"

Women hung laundry on ropes strung between trees and one boy stood straight as a spear in a faded green Boston Celtics T-shirt. He smiled and said, "Good evening. How are you?" in perfect English, which made me instinctively answer, "Great, how are you?"

He didn't respond.

One of the school buildings had the words "Lust for Ivory" painted on the outside, a remnant of colonial times when the space was used to store harvested elephant tusks, Salu told us. Another room had wooden desks, each painted with the words "Donated by Vanessa and Brian," or whatever the name of the benefactor. There were dozens. A chalkboard at the front of the room displayed simple math equations.

On the back wall, a piece of white, lined paper was taped and labeled "English Marks" with a list of names and corresponding grades. I wondered which belonged to that boy in the Celtic's T-shirt and hoped he'd passed with flying colors.

I asked another boy lingering about the school if I could snap his photo. He struck a pose in a classroom doorway, aiming his piercing eyes at my lens. I smiled thinking of the dozens of other travelers who'd probably gone through this same routine, and then I showed him the image on my digital camera screen. He smiled when he saw himself.

"*Asante*," he said. Thank you.

This would be a priceless souvenir from the expensive "thank you" trip I was on.

The medical clinic was sobering. There had been no electricity since the solar panels broke months earlier, and wasps the size of humming birds hovered, their nests clinging like barnacles to the corners of the paint-chipped examination rooms. Any desire for an aseptic environment left out the open, screenless windows. Placards posted on the walls listed the symptoms of malaria. We were told it cost $10 for a good mosquito net. Much less money than I paid for the battalion of pills I was taking to dodge the disease.

The village doctor, about 28 years old, showed us the birthing room with its small table and familiar metal stirrups. He said at night he'd use the light of a cell phone to deliver a baby. Painkillers and clean linen, he added, were hard to come by. I thought about the day my daughter was born. Equipment beeping rhythmically in my sterile room, hooked to my heart and belly signaling that all was OK with me and my baby; medicine keeping the pain at bay; a pride of doctors and nurses pushing and twisting knobs, caressing and gently urging my daughter into the brightly lit world before wrapping her in a clean blanket and taking her for a bath while I ate breakfast and watched the TV that clung to the corner of my birthing room.

We later sat on the shores of Lake Manyara and watched a group of children play soccer. A painted scene that blended normalcy with the illusory. Our &Beyond guide Stephen joined in. He said the staff regularly organizes soccer tournaments with the kids and a few times a year brings them in to Lake Manyara National Park. Despite the close proximity, many of the children have never seen the wild animals that I had just flown 5,000 miles across the world to view.

A friend of mine once told me that Africa made her feel like a tiny speck in a greater world. Up until my visit, I thought she meant physically smaller, but there were times in Africa where I felt less than small. More like irrelevant. Each night under the vast ceiling of the continent, I was engulfed on all sides by vast inky skies, like those silky parachutes we'd shake feverishly as kids, billowing it with air and ducking underneath. At sunset when the fiery, engorged orb sank toward the horizon, silhouetting the flat-topped Acacia trees and smearing the land and heavens in staggering streaks of red and orange, I knew of nothing more beautiful. When the stars winked and popped, I saw the kite-like outline of the Southern Cross for the first time and I wondered if Melau or those village kids ever took such exquisiteness for granted. I couldn't remember the last time I'd watched the sunset or stargazed back in California.

It rained. I could smell it in the earth and air before the drops pelted the ground in a tune that sounded like stones hitting cardboard. It tamped down the dust on the corrugated, teeth-chattering trails we were following and turned the dirt from oatmeal hued to a rusty, reddish brown. It raised the streams and filled the watering holes; it greened the already verdant new grass, and softened the earth where birds beaked for their dinner.

I stuck my hand out of the truck to capture the drops on my finger, then put them in my mouth to taste the African rain on my tongue. It tasted different falling from unpolluted skies. Innocent. Pure. Hopeful. That night we watched puffy clouds flicker like depleting light bulbs. The thunder wailed and shook me from the inside.

"It's not enough to just see Africa," Melau had said earlier on in our trip, referring to his continent, not just to the Serengeti where we'd stood at dusk, atop a hill overlooking miles and miles of incalculable plains.

"You must hear and smell and touch it too. Africa is to be felt."

As we flew out over Tanzania, headed back to Europe, back to home, I saw the flat top of Mount Kilimanjaro in the distance. I stared at it until I could no longer crank my head far enough to see it from the confines of my narrow window seat. Eight hours later, we landed in Amsterdam where there were no giraffes or baboons to greet us on the runway.

Some places, like some people, are felt deeper than others. I've known them. I've met them. They tunnel inside your bones and swim in your blood. They bond to your soul and awaken you from an obtuse slumber.

I now understand the yearning of that young au pair I met in Florida years ago. I miss her continent, too. And sometimes I cry.

Kimberley Lovato is a freelance writer whose work has appeared in national and international print and online media including National Geographic Traveler, American Way, Delta Sky, bbc.com, travelandleisure.com and lonelyplanet.com. Her book, Walnut Wine & Truffle Groves, won the 2012 Gold Lowell Thomas Award given by the Society of American Travel Writers Foundation, and her essays have won awards and been anthologized in several editions of Best Women's Travel Writing.(kimberleylovato.com)

MIM SWARTZ

STEPPING UP TO THE CHALLENGE
Iceland

I felt my knees go weak when I saw the warning sign about quicksand as we entered Skaftafell National Park, a gem of rugged landscape in southeast Iceland.

Quicksand forms when ice breaks away from a glacier and melts on mud or sand. It isn't always visible. That's why signs everywhere advised trekkers to stay on trails.

I took that advice seriously as we hiked about a mile to see Svartifoss, known as "Black Falls" because of its backdrop — geometrically-shaped black basalt lava columns, which can be seen throughout Iceland. Hiking hasn't been my thing — walking, yes — but here I was, climbing uphill and getting a great aerobic workout. I was wearing new hiking boots I bought just for this trip — in purple, what else, so how could I go wrong?

I confess: I am not a fearless adventurer. One of my problems is acrophobia, or fear of heights, which precludes me from attempting a lot of daring feats. Though I'm fine with heights when I'm enclosed in a safe space like an airplane or a tall building, I could never do what Nik Wallenda did recently — walk blindfolded on a tightrope (without safety net, no less) between skyscrapers in Windy City Chicago. But, then, I couldn't do any of his other equally insane stunts.

We had just come from looking at the Svinafellsjökull Glacier when I noticed another sign just outside the entrance. It, too, gave me the willies. The memorial sign was erected "with love" by families and friends of two young German tourists who had been hiking on the glacier and camping in the area in August 2007. Their tents were found, but no other trace of them.

Some of my companions went off traipsing along the edge of Svinafellsjökull. It made me jittery just watching, because I could see that the glacier was pockmarked with hundreds of ice ridges and crevasses. Guided hikes, aided by foot crampons and ice axes, were offered to crazies who wanted to peer deep into the chasms. Not happening for me. No way.

So, why did I sign up for this "Fire and Ice" tour? I guess I was looking for something to jolt me out of my comfort zone. I wanted to do things I normally wouldn't attempt. I had been to Iceland's capital city of Reykjavik several years ago, but now I wanted to see other parts of the intriguingly idyllic and sometimes eerie small volcanic island in the North Atlantic.

About two-thirds of Iceland's 320,000 inhabitants live in Reykjavik. That means visitors are apt to see more sheep than people on a drive around the island. Motorists might go for miles without encountering an oncoming car. That's a good thing on some roads off the main drag leading to nature's wonders, because they are single lane.

With three national parks geared to outdoors fanatics, I knew Iceland was the place for those more adventurous than I. But, what the heck? I was headed to Reykjavik once again for a conference, and this four-day, three-night Fire and Ice pre-tour was an option. I would be joining five people I didn't know. That was a little daunting, too. However, I had just read an essay about meeting strangers and how they can open up a new world for you. Now, I was ready to bring it on.

The part I was dreading most was riding a ski-doo snowmobile on Europe's largest ice cap, Vatnajökull, which covers about 8 percent of Iceland. I had been on a similar contraption once in Yellowstone National Park many years ago, but that ride was on groomed trails. I was sure this time would be more unnerving. I had visions of me flying off the edge of the glacier, never to be found. Would loved ones erect a memorial sign for me: "Missing since Sept. 13, 2014?"

The "ice" part of the trip was obvious — glaciers and icebergs. But what about the "fire" part? I learned that it dealt with volcanoes, some extinct and some not so much.

What I didn't know is that volcanoes are a way of life in Iceland, which has as many as 50 active volcanoes. So are earthquakes — the island has had more than 3,000 earthquakes in one month recently. The geologic activity has something to do with tectonic plates. Iceland is centered over the Mid-Atlantic Ridge, with the Eurasian plate on one side and the North American plate on the other. They're moving apart almost an inch a year.

The problem in Iceland, according to volcanologist Haraldur Sigurdsson, is that Iceland's most active volcanoes have an ice cap, and when the magma comes out under the ice at 2,500 degrees F., it melts the ice, creating violent steam explosions and massive flooding.

"If these volcanoes didn't have an ice cap, the eruptions would be quiet lava flows," he said.

I was secretly hoping that the potentially exploding volcano Bardarbunga — which was in the news constantly for weeks before my Iceland trip — would mess up things and snuff out the "fire and ice" part. But that was not to be.

To reach the start of our Vatnajökull snowmobile experience, we were shuttled from the main road in a four-wheel drive vehicle 10 miles up a steep, dirt, winding road. (I've been on these kinds of roads in my home state of Colorado, so I could handle it — not that I was crazy about the thrill.) After arriving at the base of operations, guides outfitted us with snowsuits, boots, gloves and helmets. Jon, one of the guides, asked if we would prefer to venture out on the glacier in a snowcat. We would be together in one vehicle and it would be enclosed. Not quite so scary, I thought. Sure! Of course, I was voted down.

Then I started to get cold feet — and I wasn't even on the ice yet. We had to walk down a couple hundred yards to reach the ski-doos. From my vantage point, it looked like there was a drop-off right when you reach the snow. My knees went weak again. I didn't think I would be able to make it.

"I'm not going," I told the others. I would wait in the office until they returned. Then a couple of people shouted back at me that it wasn't really that bad; the ground leveled off and there wasn't a big drop-off. So, I told myself I must do it. I must, I must, I must. I had come all this way and gotten this close — I just had to. And off I trekked to the snowmobiles.

Our group of six joined another 10 people and we paired off in twos — a driver and a passenger (that would be me) on the snowmobiles. Jon gave some instructions and told us about Vatnajökull. The ice cap is so large that five Londons would fit on it (thus, no need for me to worry about being close to the edge). But then he ruined it when he said the average crevasse on the glacier is 32 feet deep and 6 feet wide, and that he's seen crevasses up to 328 feet deep and 49 feet wide. Yikes!

"Just remember to follow me and you will get home," Jon instructed our group. Right.

Off we went, playing follow the leader, with me grabbing on tight to — OK, pulling with both hands — the back of my driver's snowsuit. Since he blocked my views some of the time, I didn't have to look at the scary parts (although it all was a little scary, especially when we bounced over bumps). But what I did see was spectacular — a huge sea of white.

And then I took Jon up on another piece of advice: relax. So, I breathed in and breathed out. And enjoyed the ride. And got home — or at least to the next adventure.

The amphibian boat ride on a nearby glacial lagoon was a piece of cake after the ski-doos on Vatnajökull — almost too tame. We climbed into the boat, which was parked on gravel and then slowly cruised its way into breathtaking Jökulsárlón, a lagoon filled with icebergs tinted blue from the play of lights and ice crystals. Icebergs constantly break off from the glacier, crash into the lagoon, wend their way to a river and eventually make their way to the Atlantic Ocean.

We kept a safe distance from the icebergs (remember the Titanic?), ogling the surreal setting in amazement. The glassy blue lagoon looked like the sky with icy jagged clouds had dropped into the water from above. It was easy to understand why Hollywood filmmakers have used the ice-filled lagoon in such movies as "A View to a Kill," "Batman Begins," "Die Another Day" and "Tomb Raider."

Willy, our on-board iceberg authority, held up a 1,000-year-old piece of ice and chopped off bits for passengers to taste. How cool.

In fact, the whole Iceland experience was amazingly cool. I was disappointed — rather than relieved — that the Fire & Ice part of my trip was coming to a close.

The trepedations I had initially were for naught. The strangers I had shared four adventurous days with were now friends. They high-fived me after each energizing encounter I thought I didn't have the guts to tackle.

I discovered a lot about myself. Who knows? Maybe next time I'll even strap on foot crampons and pick up an ice axe so I can peer deep into the chasms. I said, maybe.

Mim Swartz, an award-winning former travel editor of the Rocky Mountain News in Denver and The Denver Post, lives in Golden, CO.

DAN LEETH

GIRDING THE GLOBE
Around the World

Jet-lagged and cranky, I lingered more than two hours in line waiting to trade my passport for a cabin key. When I finally unlocked my shipboard stateroom, I found the quarters dolefully furnished in a '50s motif of faded Formica and stuffed Naugahyde. It reminded me of the Bates Motel in Hitchcock's "Psycho."

I would have chanced a shower, but my luggage hadn't yet arrived. It seemed to be as lost as Jimmy Hoffa, interred in a mausoleum of satchels, duffels, trunks and suitcases that stood floor-to-ceiling in the reception area.

Just when I thought it couldn't get worse, I learned that the executive chef was English. I envisioned four months of dining on kidney pies while waiting for clean underwear to arrive.

Such was the inauspicious start to my trip of a lifetime — a dream cruise around the world that even now, many years later, still sticks in my mind.

Since Ferdinand Magellan captained the first globe-encircling voyage in 1519, travelers have longed to circumnavigate the planet by sea. Several firms offered world cruises. Itineraries varied, but most had one commonality — they are palatially expensive.

Then along came the now-defunct World Cruise Company. By chartering older vessels and abridging amenities, the Toronto-based outfitter planned to offer around-the-world voyages at down-to-earth prices. With rates starting at about $100 per day, a lifelong fantasy could become reality. From Athens we were to sail along North Africa, steam across the Atlantic and drop down the east coast of South America. After nipping Antarctica, the cruise was to turn north and traverse Chile's fjord country before turning toward Polynesia.

But nightmares came first. Needle-jabbing nurses used my arms as immunization pincushions. I had to order extra passport pages and a slew of advance visas. Suitcases needed to be packed, unpacked and repacked until they squeaked under airline weight limitations. Ultimately, hurried good-byes and a flight to Greece led to one long-anticipated moment.

Along with 600 others, I boarded the Ocean Explorer I in Athens. After a frustrating initiation, the journey began.

Tunis, capital of Tunisia, became our first port of call. Formerly controlled by the French, this North African coastal city offers European-style prosperity springing from Arab, Roman and Phoenician roots. Islamic but liberal, Tunis is where sheiks come to be sinful.

A tour guide led us through the ruins of Carthage, a Phoenician city so old it had been sacked by the Romans before the birth of Christ. Next came the Bardo Museum and its collection of ancient mosaics. For one shopper, this was too much sightseeing. She dashed into the museum's bookshop in a desperate quest for souvenirs. To pay, she flashed American cash. When the clerk said he could only accept Tunisian dinars, the woman became indignant.

"I can't believe they won't take real money," she moaned.

"This is a foreign country," I suggested. "I doubt Barnes & Noble takes Tunisian currency back home."

Exiting the Mediterranean, we passed Prudential's Rock of Gibraltar on our way to Casablanca, Morocco. There, I signed up for a 12-hour bus trip to Marrakech, a vibrant city whose buildings echo the ruddiness of desert clay. As we wended our way there across the Saharan emptiness, our tour guide, Mohammed, bragged how Islamic men could have up to four wives. Eventually, one of the passengers had enough.

"That's nothing," the man shouted. "In North America, there is no limit to the number of wives we can have."

"Really?" Mohammed looked puzzled.

"Sure. We just have them one at a time."

Serial polygamy was even promoted onboard the ship. A plaque on the bridge assured potential newlyweds that marriages performed onboard lasted only for the duration of the cruise.

This ship's initial passengers did not have such options. Built in 1944, the vessel began its life as an American troopship hauling soldiers to World War II. Since then it had been refitted and refurbished into an ocean liner.

Old enough for AARP membership, the craft showed its age. Plumbing sputtered and ventilation wheezed. Threadbare carpets revealed years of stains, and paint barely concealed bathroom rust. The shabby conditions caused some to cancel passage and leave in disgust. Others shared their unhappiness, whining to anyone who would listen. I took it all in stride. For what we were paying, I could not expect opulence. Besides, the scruffiness reminded me of home.

On day 10 we reached the Canary Islands, a Spanish beach playground off Africa's northwest coast. Rather than take a tour, I opted to spend the day sauntering solo through the port city of Santa Cruz de Tenerife. Its sidewalk cafes, fountained parks and shady promenades provided a refreshing touch of Europe. Even though most places took dollars, I found an ATM and bought local currency. It felt liberating to escape fellow passengers.

Unfortunate for my waistline, one of my initial fears proved unfounded. The meals cooked by our English chef tasted fine, although some dishes were not what one expected. This especially applied to desserts. The tollhouse cookies, for example, contained nary a chocolate chip, and the pumpkin pie was best described as, "It sort of tastes yellow."

The worst culinary disaster was the coffee. The muck brewed onboard came from beans that must have been ground beneath Juan Valdez's mule before being dumped aboard as bilge ballast. Greenpeace never would have allowed this foul substance to be spilled overboard for fear of killing whales.

Our last stop in the eastern Atlantic was Cape Verde, a former Portuguese island colony located off the coast of Senegal. In slave-trading days, African natives came through here on their way to Brazil.

Many of us crammed into pregnant minivans for an all-day, cross-island tour. In spite of cheek-to-cheek seating, the trip proved delightful. The island's arid, volcanic landscape reminded me of Arizona. Everywhere we drove, smiling, colorfully dressed residents stood by their homes and waved. Best of all, we did more sightseeing than shopping. It was a perfect "guy trip."

For six full days we crossed the Atlantic, and as it was throughout the journey, the time at sea was pure pleasure. Professional lecturers and retired professors gave talks about the science, culture and history of the places we visited. Passengers and staff taught classes on writing, dancing, painting and more. Between brain stimulations, there was time for reading, sunbathing and swimming.

At sunset, some poured drinks and gathered on deck. Eyes gazed westward in hopes of catching the elusive "green flash," a teal burst that can occur when the top of the solar disk touches the horizon. Those with stronger drinks claimed more sightings.

After dark, some of us searched for the Southern Cross. Others retreated to the lounges where musicians performed everything from Frankie Avalon to Frank Zappa. The ship's theater offered standard cruise-fare stage productions featuring magicians, comedians, cabaret singers or concert pianists. We even had guest speakers onboard.

Salvador became our first Brazilian port. Built on cliffs, this former colonial center features a color-splashed historical district. As I wandered around, a school-age boy approached. In his native Portuguese, he told me what I was looking at, but I failed to comprehend a single word.

"*Obrigado*," I thanked him, and walked on.

He followed, intent on providing a guided tour. Assuming he was freelancing, I offered money, but he refused the payment. The two of us continued through town. He explained the sights in his local language. I responded as best I could in a meld of pidgin Portuguese and Taco Bell Spanish. He grinned, graciously pretending to understand.

On world cruises, most port stops last only one day, and plans can be dashed if the weather proves uncooperative. Such was the case in Rio de Janeiro.

We arrived on Sunday, and I had hoped to go birding. Our onboard aviary expert said Rio's sugar-sand beaches should be rife with curvaceous, string-bottomed chickadees. Unfortunately, gloomy drizzle greeted our arrival, and the only species I spotted were gaggles of Speedo-briefed beach roosters strutting plump plumage on shoreline volleyball courts.

Buenos Aires proved much sunnier. Parks, monuments and outdoor cafés fill Argentina's colorful and cosmopolitan capital. Here, fabric shrinkage seemed to be endemic. I encountered hundreds of young women whose apparel fit so tightly that if they had a peso in their pockets, I could read the year it was minted. It's no surprise that anorexia is rampant in this Paris of the South.

The windswept Falkland Islands became our first English-speaking port. Looking at the barren landscape, I wondered how anyone but the British could desire such a desolate outpost.

But the Argentines apparently did. More than three decades ago, their soldiers invaded the Falklands, battling the English in what one reporter said was akin to two bald men fighting over a comb. Temporarily victorious, the first thing the Argentines did was require traffic to drive on the right side of the road. A few months later, the British liberated the islands and restored left-lane motoring.

Steaming south, we crossed the Drake Passage, the 600-mile gap between South America and Antarctica that is billed as the roughest water on earth. Passengers downed Dramamine, wrapped wristbands and plastered on patches, all in a desperate attempt to alleviate seasickness. Only when we reached frigid Antarctica did seas and stomachs calm.

In the South Shetlands, inflatable Zodiac boats unloaded us on a rocky Antarctic beach. There, we watched 3-ton elephant seals lounge like lard-bellied couch potatoes while tuxedoed penguins strutted by like midget maître d's.

In the cool of Antarctica, our geezerly ship showed its years. A few cabins received enough heat to turn them into Finnish saunas. The ducts in mine, however, exhaled less warmth than a zombie's breath. I kept hoping the menopausal heating system would have a hot flash, but it never did.

We recrossed the Drake, passed Cape Horn and headed into the Beagle Channel off the island of Tierra del Fuego. After stops in Ushuaia, Argentina, the southernmost city in the world, we continued through the Straits of Magellan and on to Punta Arenas, Chile.

On day 48 we headed up the Patagonian coast through the incomparable Chilean fjord country. Its dark passages dripped with glaciers, ice chutes and waterfalls. Although temperatures hovered slightly above freezing, I spent as much time as possible on deck. With no cabin heat, it felt cozier outside.

As we turned to cross the Pacific, the journey dove to a low. Not only was the room colder than my ex-wife's stare, but the coffee quality tumbled from ghastly to worse. Rather than using beans, the cooks began making the brew from bottled syrup that resembled crankcase-drained Pennzoil. I sipped the loathsome liquid only for warmth. Fortunately, Polynesia loomed ahead.

The ship reeled, its course pummeled by the dual punches of the Humboldt Current meeting a South Pacific gale. Spray flew as the bow jabbed and lurched through churning swells. Passengers staggered, dishes tumbled, and lunches were lost in more ways than one.

From the safety of my cabin, I gazed awestruck at Neptune's fury. Turbulent days like this were part of the adventure of cruising around the world.

On the journey's 55th day, we reached Easter Island. This was our first overnight stop, and many passengers seized the opportunity to sleep ashore. For once, we could dine on fresh seafood and sip coffee that didn't taste like Jiffy Lube sludge.

Mysterious stone effigies called *moai* have made Easter Island famous. Sculpted centuries ago, these statues can stand 32 feet tall and weigh 80 tons or more. Scientists have debated why primitive Polynesians carved the *moai* and erected them around the island. Personally, I believe it was a preliterate Chamber of Commerce ploy to reward us tourists for journeying to the most isolated isle on earth.

Easter Island's nearest inhabited neighbor, Pitcairn Island, lies 1,200 miles away. On this 2-square-mile hunk of rock, mutineers from the Bounty came to hide in 1790. Fifty of their descendants still live there. We were to go ashore, but rough seas precluded a landing.

Since we could not visit the island, the islanders came to us. They brought goods to sell — clothes, carvings, books, stamps, postcards and even plaques bearing scraps of the HMS Bounty. A shopping orgy exploded on deck. When the spree finally ended, the islanders held wads of green and the ship looked like a Pitcairn Island T-shirt emporium.

Although every age cohort was represented onboard, the majority of our passengers had long been receiving Social Security checks. While the kids behaved like grown-ups, many of the adults acted like spoiled adolescents. They squabbled, bickered, fussed and complained about everything from saving seats to tipping.

The biggest problem, however, was theft. Personal property seemed safe, but items belonging to the ship or staff vanished with regularity. Passengers ripped out sections of guidebooks for their own use. Someone pilfered the VCR used by instructors, then allegedly threw it overboard. Reference materials and dictionaries disappeared from the ship's library, while maps and notices vanished from walls. One brazen thief even stooped to swipe tinsel from the ship's chaplain.

We soon sampled the siren isles of the South Pacific. In Tahiti, I rented a car and explored the land that inspired Gauguin and drove the Bounty crewmen to mutiny. As I pedaled a bicycle around Bora Bora, locals greeted me with smiling *bonjours*. In the Fiji Museum, I saw cannibal forks used at a 19th-century dinner party whose guest of honor and main entrée was a Methodist missionary. Off New Caledonia, I got a double feature as I snorkeled near a catamaran on which several bikini-clad lasses lounged. Below the surface, it was "A Fish Called Wanda." Above, it looked like out-takes from "Baywatch."

A torrential downpour dampened our arrival to Australia's Great Barrier Reef. There I discovered that snorkeling in a deluge could be fun, in spite of a chilling, pelting rain-driven back massage.

Near Darwin on Australia's north coast, I took a river tour to see man-eating crocodiles. I had high expectations, but the guide said we would not be allowed to toss disgruntled passengers to the toothy reptiles.

Actually, most of my shipmates were pleasant to be around, and after months of prison-close confinement, we knew each other by face if not by name. With some I bonded well. Others I found as endearing as in-laws and prayed we would never cross paths again. They probably felt the same.

Bali, my favorite shipmates' favorite port, came next. On this Indonesian island, rice paddies terrace volcanic hillsides, sacred monuments rise Godward, dinner can be had for $5, and everywhere the people seemed honest and genuinely amicable. Friendly, sacred, scenic and cheap, I had to agree Bali offered a touch of paradise.

The biggest deterrents to enjoying the island were the hoards of vendors who greeted our arrival. As I stepped ashore, a clutch of walking Walmarts swarmed me like flies heading for a steaming cow-pie. These sidewalk salespeople proffered blue-light specials such as three T-shirts for $10, four ball caps for $5 and "genuine" Rolex wristwatches at two for $15. Show interest in their products and they latched on like swamp mosquitoes slurping a nudist. I was lucky to escape solvent.

After stops in Java and Singapore we hit Sri Lanka, the island nation southeast of India. The country was enduring an ethnic civil war, but our main danger was not bullets and bombs. It was deadly traffic. I spent a white-knuckled day riding with shipmates to the interior to see the ruins of Sigiriya. There, a 5th-century ruler, who also feared for his life, built a stronghold atop a 600-foot-tall stone monolith. At least he had 500 dancing concubines to allay his worries.

Residents of the Maldives have a wetter fear. The highest point in their chain of atolls towers only 6 feet above the Indian Ocean. If global warming causes seas to rise, these folks may have to snorkel to bed.

After calling on the mountainous Seychelles Islands, the ship docked for three days in Mombasa, Kenya. Many passengers departed for brief game safaris. A friend and I opted instead for an overnight visit to the Tanzanian island of Zanzibar.

We spent an afternoon exploring Stone Town, a timeworn Arab seaport that once served as the capital of Oman. Small shops lined narrow streets, and vintage buildings bore exotic carved doors.

The following morning, we took a taxi to a preserve for Zanzibar red colobus monkeys, one of Africa's rarest primates. Locals call them poison monkeys and believe that after the animals feed in an area, plants and crops will die. For the hour we watched them flit through trees, the only thing dying was time.

Our driver dropped us at the airport for our return flight to Mombasa. We secured boarding passes and seat assignments, then paid departure taxes and cleared immigration. Finally came security check.

A military officer directed us one at a time to an armed soldier who stood behind a small table. My friend went first. He opened his bags, talked, smiled and left for the departure lounge. The directing guard then sent me to the soldier.

"You have Tanzanian shillings left?" he asked.

"No, I exchanged no money here," I honestly answered.

"Then you give me one dollar," he said.

I immediately understood. This was the baksheesh shakedown table. I looked at the soldier. I looked at his gun. I looked down the hallway to the strip-search examination room.

Without hesitation, I pulled a single from my pocket and slipped it to the soldier. He smiled and sent me on my way. The man never did check my bag for guns, bombs or contraband.

The journey's most touching stop may have been Eritrea, an impoverished nation on the Horn of Africa. Well off the tourist track, it gets fewer visitors per year than some McDonald's restrooms get in one day. With 600 onboard, our arrival became a national event.

A group of white-scarved women greeted the ship, dancing and chanting with the verve of hoedowners at a backwoods revival. Uniformed schoolchildren presented floral bouquets to the cruise director and her assistants. A videographer filmed our arrival for Eritrean television, and reporters interviewed passengers as they toured the countryside. Either we were the biggest event to hit Eritrea since its liberation from Ethiopia, or this was a very slow news day.

At the Jordanian port of Aqaba, four of us hired a taxi to drive to Petra, the 2,300-year-old Nabataean city carved into the walls of a desert canyon. The driver agreed to $120 for the day. At journey's end, he demanded $250, claiming he provided "extras." The up-charge must have been for thrills he provided by playing chicken with oncoming traffic.

When we refused to yield to the gouging, the scene became ugly. Both sides threatened to call the police. Finally, we plopped $120 on the pavement and walked toward the ship. I kept glancing over my shoulder, half expecting to see squad cars and flashing lights. I just hoped Jordanian jails served decent coffee.

The World Cruise Company's inaugural voyage was drawing to a close. By now, most of us had forgiven the ship's shoddiness. The pain of heatless rooms and slow-draining showers had been more than offset by the journey's extraordinary itinerary and education program.

Unfortunately, negative feedback eroded confidence back home. In spite of prices starting at about $100 per day, bookings for the second cruise faltered. When fuel costs tripled, the company was doomed. Our journey went full term. The follow-up cruise on a different vessel folded mid-route. The idea of offering budget-priced, around-the-world voyages seems viable. Perhaps another company will continue the practice.

We sailed through the Suez Canal and stopped in Israel, our final port before Greece. I took a tour to Jerusalem. Ambling through the ancient walled city, I felt the holy auras of Islam, Judaism and Christianity. Before heading back to the ship, the bus made a rest stop at a small cafe and gift shop. It was called the Elvis Inn.

I had covered 27,646 nautical miles and explored 33 ports in 25 countries. Now I stood in perhaps the most revered city on earth. There before me, shadowed in the halo of the late day sun, rose a towering statue of Elvis.

Transfixed in humbled awe, I gazed into the eyes of the gilded icon from Graceland.

Suddenly, everything made sense. It was time to go home.

Dan Leeth, who lives in Aurora, CO, is a full-time travel writer and photographer whose words and images have graced newspapers, magazines and books across the United States and Canada. See more at danleeth.com and lookingfortheworld.com.

GINA KREMER

PARADISE LOST
Hawaii, USA

As I raced to the airport to catch my midnight flight, I tried to ignore the sharp stinging all over my body. My duffle bag cut into my shoulder, and my back ached. I was exhausted and shocked at how my 11-day vacation in Hawaii had ended.

My first five blissful days on Maui had been focused on a friend's paradise wedding. There had been lots of special time with the bride, taking in cocktails by the infinity pool and pampering for a seaside wedding celebration.

After the newlyweds departed to Kauai for their honeymoon, I decided to stay on Maui and explore. Through stateside mutual friends before the trip, I was introduced to Nat, a Maui local.

My short e-mail exchanges with Nat offered a glimpse of our respective personalities. I knew he was a naturopathic physician who also sang and played guitar in a band. He knew I was an outdoorsy and independent free spirit looking for adventure.

When we met for dinner, I immediately felt a sense of trust and camaraderie, which quickly progressed to friendly ribbing and biting sarcasm.

I didn't know it then, but that night we set the plan for the biggest adventure of my life.

It all started with a simple statement.

"I think you would like the Commando Hike," said Nat.

"What's that?" I asked.

"It's a really hard trail. But you can't chicken out if you try it."

On most occasions, the fastest way to get me to do anything is to insinuate that I can't do it. Like a moth to a flame, I accepted the challenge.

"You're on."

We were set to do the Commando Hike on Saturday afternoon, the day of my departure.

In the 48 hours leading up to the hike, I squeezed in a week of tourist activity.

I drove the famous 600-turn road to Hana, slept at Koki Beach, found a hidden red sand beach in Hana, checked out the caves and black sand beach at Waianapanapa State Park, dangled 3,500 feet in the air from a motorized hang glider, hiked the Pipiwai Trail to a 200-foot waterfall, swam in the Seven Sacred Pools, drove up to the Haleakala Crater at sunset, and stared at the stars on the front of my car with a flask of whiskey. After seeing the sunrise at Haleakala, I caught breakfast in Kula and drank a morning mai tai in Paia, Maui's famous hippie surfer town.

When Saturday rolled around, I was wiped out. But there were no earlier flights, and I didn't want to sit on the beach.

The Commando Hike it was.

"It takes an hour to get there, the hike is about two hours, then one hour back," Nat explained.

I had a flight at 11:30 p.m. and he had a wedding at 5 p.m. We were on a strict timetable.

After trailing along countless turns and navigating numerous one-lane bridges among vibrant scenery, we pulled up to a nondescript roadside fence. No signage, nothing. You could have passed by without a second thought.

After chugging water to stay hydrated, we set out with Nat as my guide. Packing light, we only had water shoes and a headlamp for the caves.

We enjoyed a sunshine-filled stroll among the grass and were greeted by a golden brown cow grazing next to us. I found it strange that even in the vacation postcard island of Maui, cows were ever-present. In fact, cows and horses grazing on the edge of sea cliffs is completely normal in Maui.

Along our walk, Nat plucked strawberry guavas for us to eat, while painted eucalyptus trees greeted us. Our path then led to a stream. The 10-foot-wide stream was edged in lush, thick greenery and offered countless rocks to hop on.

As I danced from rock to rock, tall trees with winding limbs and rope-like vines surrounded us among a parade of shrubbery and greenery. There are no bald patches in the Hawaiian jungle. It is thick, dense and topped with a canopy.

Algae-covered rocks threatened to challenge our balance, but we trudged on. After half an hour, the stream became enveloped in thick tree roots and branches. We started jumping over thigh-high foliage as thick as our fists.

Next, we hit deeper pools of water. Climbing in, the water rose with each step.

To keep going, we would need to complete a short vertical rock climb up sharp gray rock. A waterfall trickled directly in our path, and our fingers grasped wet rock as we ascended. The rocks were sharp, but offered enough grips to keep going. As I rose to the top, a cave came into view.

I squealed with excitement. A wet cave made from an ancient lava tube? We don't get those at home

We swam toward the cave and began the ascent inside. The first pool was waist high, as was the next.

After another shallower pool, the fourth pool brought us deeper into the cave. The light behind us grew dim, and nothing but darkness lay before us.

Excitement and a tinge of fear pushed me onward. As I pulled myself over the next rock threshold, I plunged into deeper waters and swam into the blackness.

Swimming across, a sliver of light began to enter into view from above. The way out.

Climbing up slick rock accented by a dribbling waterfall, we used our touch as a guide.

Arriving at the top of the cave, we walked with hunched backs toward the light. As we approached, I saw that the glamorous ending to our adventure was an irrigation system that required shimmying through thick, rusted metal bars.

Back outside, a large pool of water lay before us.

"What is the way out?" I asked.

"Right there in front of us."

It was another waterfall and rock face combination, and while it looked intimidating, I had made it this far. Why worry now?

But as we swam closer, I realized how tall it was, and how slick. Could I climb 15 feet up through these obstacles?

The handholds we had in the cave had now been replaced by larger expanses of smooth, wet rock. On the left side the rock wall inverted, offering vines and tree limbs as the only options. The middle was right through a small waterfall. The far right offered a limited amount of climbing options that required large steps with scarce handholds.

One wrong move and you would fall backward, hitting the rocks below before falling into the water.

Nat explored the options and determined the left route was the safest route. It would require skillful fingers and solid upper body strength.

In my life I have proved strength and endurance many times, but never with my upper body.

I wasn't keen on cracking my head on a rock in the middle of nowhere, so I suggested a safer and less exciting route out.

"Why not bushwhack?"

Finding our way back to the beginning couldn't be that hard. It would be easier to walk through the jungle than go through the entire hike again backward.

As we swam across to the beginning of the pool to get to shallower ground, we vaguely plotted our route. We had to go around the back of the waterfall before us and then back toward where we had started. To do so, we first had to cut a large circle on the right.

We started on our way, and I enjoyed my up-close view of the rainforest.

I'd never seen anything like it.

Dr. Seuss-like plants grew in all directions, looping toward the sky. Like nature's shag carpeting, moss lay in a rainbow of lime, sage, green and banana yellow at tree bases. Tree limbs wound in all directions, draping vines to the ground in their path. Green foliage poured out of rich bark in waxy, cascading ribbons.

Looking up, a canopy sheltered us from direct sunlight and looked like a sunlit green snowflake. Ferns, shrubs, saplings and moss multiplied exponentially into the distance before my eyes.

I was in heaven.

The downside to a dense jungle environment is that navigating a straight line is impossible.

Going straight may need to be accomplished by first going right, curving left, then right again.

The next hour ensued with us bushwhacking through grass as tall as our shoulders, climbing over large trees, ducking under low-lying branches, and snacking on strawberry guava while we skirted a stream.

We had changed direction so many times, I had no idea where we had started.

After heading up a ridge and descending down, we found ourselves on top of a 40-foot dropoff to a shallow, rocky pool below.

We headed back up to find the next gulch. The canopy was so dense and vast, we couldn't take a peek from above and get a solid view of where we were going.

Nat stayed calm and confident, so I stayed hopeful. My mind drifted to the sushi dinner I hoped to have soon. But my mind also wondered — didn't all bad horror flicks start out like this?

We spent another hour climbing through the forest and following "trails." He called them trails, but I wouldn't call them that. A trail is marked. A trail has been frequented. A trail leads to a destination. Everything we followed ended in a dead end.

Using the ridge as a guide, Nat estimated we were close. The ridgeline was descending to the level of the painted eucalyptus trees where we had started.

As we trekked on, we listened closely for the two sounds to lead us — cars and cattle. Where they were, flat land waited.

We had started at the road, but with the winding roads of Maui, it was hard to gauge the location of the sound. I could have sworn the horrific cattle moans were a cow giving birth, but Nat assured me that it was a little something called bovine sexual healing.

Cattle mooed and shrieked in the distance, and we tried to gauge their direction in order to follow. But cattle are always in motion. We couldn't trust them to guide us.

As we walked, we discovered what must have been an equipment holding area for illegal marijuana growers, long since forgotten. Plastic watering containers and disintegrated plastic lay cracked in the burrow of a tree trunk.

Maybe he was right. Maybe these were trails after all?

Although a couple of hours had passed, I stayed calm.

I could hear cattle and cars, but it was taking forever to get near them. We couldn't tell if the sound was straight ahead or reflecting off an obstruction. After much debate, we agreed that the sound was coming from the right.

I didn't want to feel defeated by the situation. I had done the Commando Hike, after all, and conquered plenty of outdoor adventures in my past. I was going to become one with this damn rainforest and find my way out.

Reaching into the mud below me, I dug in two fingers and painted two lines across my cheeks. Nature's war paint. Bring it on.

After scrambling, our explorations led us to a small trickling stream with a 15-foot steep tangle of hau trees on top.

We determined that if we followed the stream, we would be headed toward safety. But to do that, we had to climb over, under and through the web of hau trees to move forward. With renewed optimism and hope, I eagerly grabbed on to the branches around me.

We felt like monkeys — although we moved with the grace and dexterity of an elderly, blind monkey couple. But still, we were monkeys nonetheless.

We climbed forward through a sharp and twisted web of hau, catching our faces, arms and legs in the branches along the way.

Vines and branches pulled at my clothes and threatened to trap my legs. My right shoe opened up in the front, and the sole was pulled out after getting stuck in the branches. I heard an audible rip as Nat's shorts snagged on a branch. The entire left flap on the rear of his shorts had torn open. I'm sure the draft he felt across his backside was unnerving.

I thought of a friend who had made it a point to hug a tree to feel more connected to the earth. I chuckled to myself, thinking about all the trees I was hugging. Hell, I was a tree-hugging slut. I couldn't possibly be more connected to the earth right now.

All the while, I was being eaten by every mosquito along the way. Sometimes the branches were thick and provided a solid web to perch upon while planning the next move, other times they were smaller, with nothing but green canopy above us and nothing to grasp.

There was safety to be found in climbing atop the web; there were a hundred limbs to catch you on your way down. But that also meant there were a hundred small sharp broken branches waiting to pierce flesh.

Nat spotted more rainbow eucalyptus trees ahead. We were getting closer.

After two hours climbing through hau trees, the sun started to fade. My calm began to crack. For the first time, I contemplated the obvious — we may not get out before sunset.

Inside, I felt a mixture of fear and resentment brewing. I had agreed and trusted him, but I did not sign up for this. And it wasn't until after starting he confessed that he had only completed the hike once.

I now had my fate tied to the hands of a man I barely knew

Nat stayed calm and reassuring. He kept asking if I was OK, and was obviously trying his best. He didn't want to be in this situation either.

Discord is a recipe for disaster. We had to stay unified, and I had to stay calm. It was comforting to know that Nat was a doctor, and if anything happened, I would be in good hands. But if something happened to him, what would I do? I put the thought out of my mind.

"Whatever you do, be careful. We can't get injured right now. Take it slow and test each branch," he advised.

I tried my best, but as the final traces of sunlight drained from the sky, the branches became harder and harder to see.

All we had leading us was a faulty headlamp that had been submerged in water. Without that light, we were toast. It could go out at any minute. Whenever I stood on the branches and contemplated my next move, my legs shook. My arms and stomach burned from hoisting myself up and over so many obstacles.

Then I saw a patch of green to the right. We had heard cows and cars to the right. Why not give it a try?

As we got closer to the green patch, we were now immersed in total darkness. We couldn't see stars; the foliage above us was too thick. We slid our bodies along the ground underneath the trees, the stream was now gone.

Standing up, a thick bamboo forest began ahead of us. Finally, we could stand on the ground and walk straight. I could have cried for joy.

We embraced in relief, then charged toward the direction we hoped was the car.

There was a clear-cut path to follow through the bamboo, and within minutes we had reached a clearing. We could see the stars in the sky above us.

His headlamp illuminated what looked like a bridge.

We stepped hastily forward, and within minutes we found the road. We had made it.

"We did it! We're out! We're free!" I said.

His voice took on a serious tone.

"I didn't want to tell you while we were back there, but that was really serious. People die in situations like that all the time."

I knew we had been close, but I hadn't wanted to contemplate how close. After six hours, we were bruised, scraped, bloody, sore, bitten — but we were alive.

"You should search online for Commando Hike trail deaths and see what you find," said Nat.

"If I would have thought of that, I wouldn't have gone," I retorted, punching his arm.

Who was I kidding? I still would have gone. Curiosity is a dangerous drug.

During a hot shower at Nat's house, I gingerly removed caked dirt and sanitized my wounds. He got ready to make an appearance at the wedding reception before it ended. I packed for my flight. We said our final goodbyes.

"I won't ever forget you or what we went through today. You're tough," he said.

It was certainly a hike I would never forget. Collapsing into the airplane seat, I never felt so grateful and safe.

Travel writer Gina Kremer of Denver has an insatiable thirst for adventure and a self-diagnosed case of chronic wanderlust that can get her into trouble. During her travels she has clumsily tripped onto the northern side of the military demarcation line in South Korea, flown with strangers in a puddle jumper to a secluded Bahamian island party, strapped on crampons to hike glaciers in Iceland, and accidentally driven through private vineyards in Italy. Whether it's hiking 1,400 miles on the Appalachian Trail, drinking whiskey and making new friends in Scotland, or roaming Burning Man on a cruiser bike, she is up for it.

DARRIN DUFORD

LIONFISH QUEST
Belize

The burbles and pops of something frying grew louder, and so did the conflicting thoughts. Sitting across from my wife at an outdoor wooden table on Belize's sandy Ambergris Caye, I was considering the conspicuous appearance of the lionfish. You can't miss it: The fish's long, feathery fins complement its venomous dorsal spines that thrust out like a Mayan headdress. It seems more drawn than grown. It's the kind of haunting attractiveness you expect to find in endangered species, something that would be coveted for aquariums while its organs are carved up for black-market aphrodisiacs.

And I had just paid good money to eat it.

So had everyone else at the tables of the open-air Pirate's Treasure Restaurant. While still popular in home aquariums, the lionfish is not endangered. Nor does its liver find its way into love potions. Originally from the

Western Pacific and the Indian Ocean, it is invasive in Caribbean waters, and is gobbling up native reef fish and mollusks with gruesome relentlessness. Each lionfish can consume prey up to half its size, a Joey Chestnut of the sea. They can mate every four days, and one female can produce two million eggs per year.

The lionfish, however, also happens to mate well with a dusting of flour and a deep fryer.

The idea of targeting invasive species with a dinner fork has gained attention since science writer James Gorman coined the term "invasivore" in a 2010 piece for The New York Times titled "A Diet for an Invaded Planet." (The lionfish is the first species Gorman mentions.) The nonnative wild boar of the American South often end up in sausage casings; restaurateur and James Beard Award nominee Bun Lai devotes a page in his menu to invasive species at his New Haven sushi restaurant.

Louisiana chefs have experimented with the levee-wrecking nutria, a furry, 12-pound vegetarian rodent originally from South America, but with limited success owing to the rodent stigma that holds back nutria from its full potential as an entrée. Being recognizable as a fish, the lionfish doesn't suffer from such taxonomical hang-ups.

While lionfish has been turning up on menus across Belize's coast, the Pirate's Treasure Restaurant, connected to a series of bungalows called the Pirate Villas, is the only restaurant in Belize that serves lionfish as its only fish.

"Ninety percent of my customers order lionfish," owner Jason Gilbertson told us, "so I had to get rid of snapper." Gilbertson is an Atlanta transplant whose Belizean girlfriend, Maresha Reid, is the restaurant's head chef. Her specialty: piña colada lionfish, which, despite sounding like a very unserious dish, is actually quite wonderful.

The fish has a sweet caramelized coating from spending a night in a marinade of piña colada before being flambéed (Reid uses the whole drink, according to Gilbertson). Its flesh is firm but still moist and surrenders willingly to the bite. At the same time, its flavor only differs in degree but not kind from other edible fish, making it an ideal ingredient for experimentation.

Jason gave us a lift back to San Pedro in his golf cart — the island's de facto transportation. His dog Pirate, part pit-bull and part Labrador retriever, lay at his feet. As he navigated the cart around puddles in the dirt street, I asked him how he obtains the lionfish, since no other restaurant in San Pedro I had approached was serving it.

"I have divers on call," he told us, a cigarette in the corner of his mouth ashing when we rode over the bumps. His divers employ the most effective method to date, using spear guns to pluck the invaders from the reef one by one. The diving team free dives and can spear about 100 pounds of lionfish per outing, providing Reid with 30 to 40 pounds of fillets.

Spearfishing for venomous creatures while holding one's breath sounded like a challenging method of cleaning up the reef. I wanted to see how it was done.

I got my chance the following week in Hopkins, a hot, flat town spread along the center of Belize's coastline, where I'd find that the only thing separating me from venom and agony was a disposable plastic bottle.

*****

The lionfish's joyride through the Caribbean and Western Atlantic began in 1992, when, according to legend at least, Hurricane Andrew smashed at least one waterfront aquarium in Florida containing lionfish. Regulation has not yet caught up with the lionfish's appetite, and its appeal to the aquarium enthusiast has not waned. On a recent check of the website of an American pet store chain, I noticed that the same species of lionfish that is ravaging Caribbean and Western Atlantic reefs, Pterois volitans, is still available with the caveat "Will eat any tankmate that can fit in its mouth."

From those beginnings, it has already spread as far north as the Carolinas — not counting the odd, hopefully anomalous sighting off the coast of Rhode Island — and as far west as Belize, as far south as Panama and as far east as St. Croix.

Native Caribbean predators such as the grouper and moray eel don't recognize lionfish as prey, unless the lionfish is injured. Some juvenile fish think the lionfish's plumage is cover in which to hide. Meanwhile, the lionfish recognizes any number of Caribbean reef fish as snacks.

The lionfish's nature as a predator may seem contradictory to its size — adults rarely grow longer than 15 inches. But a study by Oregon State University revealed that lionfish reduced the juvenile fish population of one reef by 79 percent in only five weeks. These are the same reefs that provide jobs to fishermen and tourist guides, and also help protect coastlines of low-lying areas from storms and tidal forces. This is no smaller matter in Belize — the former capital Belize City, home to a quarter of the country's population, lies almost entirely below sea level.

Colder sea water seems to be the only natural force stopping them in the Western Hemisphere. That leaves humans as the most promising line of defense.

*****

Mounds of coral protruded like discarded Volkswagen beetles on the sea floor. I was following the snorkel fins of fisherman and guide Noel Nuñez, who was systematically scanning the crevices in the mounds, his 3-foot spear gun gracefully extending his profile. Nuñez looks to be in his late-30s, and is of Garifuna heritage, a legacy of the descendants of Carib Amerindians who intermarried with survivors of wrecked slave ships in the 18th century.

While he was examining one side of the coral, I would examine the other, eyeing a rainbow of fish — wrasses, grunts, most of them smaller than bread plates — as they swam into covered archways under the coral mounds, into peek-a-boo channels, and around coffee-colored, elephant-ear vegetation gently flapping in the current.

After an hour of swimming near the shallows of the Blue Ground Range, part of Belize's inner reef that lies 10 miles east of Hopkins, we hadn't seen a single sprawling fin or red zebra stripe of a lionfish. Unlike other fishing trips, having a slow day of lionfishing was a good thing. Our difficulty meant that in the 10 years since Belizean fishermen first started spotting lionfish, the fishermen have already succeeded at decimating the lionfish population in the shallows. Deeper depths, however, are another story, as scuba divers regularly report that lionfish abound at a depth of around 60 feet off Belize's reefs. Several towns, including San Pedro, host lionfish spearing competitions, whose award categories include the most lionfish speared, the largest lionfish and the smallest.

In a smooth, unannounced motion, Nuñez dove under the surface and inserted his speargun into a narrow channel of a brain-shaped coral colony. A sharp snap broke the silence of the reef. He had released the trigger. He lifted the spear above the water to reveal a curled-up lionfish, wriggling for the last time. It spread out its striped fins in a slow, probing fashion and seemed confused that something had the audacity to attack it.

"How do you say 'good shot' in Garifuna?" I asked Nuñez.

"*Buiti*," he answered, briefly pausing before swimming back to the boat. The catch was small — about 7 inches — but Nuñez estimated that it was already 3 years old, two years past the age in which it had reached sexual maturity. There would be no mercy for the adolescents.

Judel, Nuñez's son, had been manning the boat while Nuñez and I snorkeled. Nuñez said something to his son in Garifuna, and Judel began cutting the top off a plastic water bottle. Judel then lifted up the lionfish from under its mouth and dropped it inside the bottle to protect us from the venomous spines. The motion was fluid, almost casual. It was not his first time bottling a lionfish.

I asked Judel, "What is your favorite recipe for lionfish?"

In his early teens, Judel had remained quiet on the ride out to the reef, dutifully taking orders from his father, but he didn't need to think about my question. "I like it fried," he said.

As Nuñez started up the outboard motor to change spots, I held the plastic bottle to keep it from tipping over. Almost as fast as the lionfish infestation began, diving companies started marketing protective gear for lionfish hunting such as puncture-resistant gloves and mesh-reinforced bags (one is nicknamed the Lionfish

Hotel). But the bottle in my hand, its brand the same as the bottle I'd sipped from at breakfast, unceremoniously rose to the task, as long as I didn't spill it.

I peered down inside the bottle. I was looking at a thing that had probably scarfed down hundreds of juvenile reef fish. Yet it was small enough so that the entire profile of its head fit sideways in the bottle. Its stubby antennae looked cartoonish. Brown and orange stripes ran under its eye, which was transparent except for a tack-like black pupil. It seemed to be frowning a child's frown, playing the cute card, as if to say, "What did I do wrong?"

I had already felt self-assured about preying on the reef's self-assured predator, but as I appreciated the creature's colors and curves up close, I realized that the killing and eating of lionfish could also safely feed a darker longing — the Fight Club-esque desire to destroy something beautiful. (The motivation, alas, has yet to be explored in the marketing materials of anti-lionfish campaigns.)

When we swam in a new spot, I employed Nuñez's crevice-scanning technique, slowly floating above and examining all angles into each opening. Inside the first crevice, down about three feet, a 1-foot lionfish was spreading its fins like a turkey, spinning leisurely. Perhaps it was hunting; the lionfish often stretches out its long fins to corner its prey. I yelled to Nuñez, who swam to me and began checking all the cave-like entries and exits in the 20-foot-wide coral mound.

After we examined each hole repeatedly, the fish did not reappear. "It's hiding," Nuñez said. We could do nothing but move on to a different spot.

Under the heavy heat of noon on the roofless boat, we nibbled on cold fried chicken thighs Nuñez had brought aboard in a cooler for lunch. I asked him if he was concerned about the lionfish's venomous spines when he free dives. While the venom is not fatal (unless the victim has an allergic reaction), the resulting pain has been known to strike acutely and can linger for days. "They'll get you good, especially when they are attacking you," he said before chewing off another bite.

"What does it feel like to be stung by a lionfish?"

His answer: "Have you ever been stung by a scorpion?"

*****

"This knife is sharp!" chirped Marley, Nuñez's oldest son, as he swung a long chef's knife onto a plywood table in his yard. The table, doubling as a cutting board, still held the remains of a coconut husk, cleanly halved, and now also held the lionfish on its side. Marley is a hip-hop music video producer, but in exchange for my assistance in helping to build his website, he had offered to clean the lionfish, a potentially dangerous task few in town would attempt. Before I had met Marley, I walked the length of the packed dirt road that serves as Hopkins' main and only drag, searching in vain for a restaurant cook who knew how to clean lionfish without getting stung.

Marley had grabbed the fish out of the plastic bottle by its head just like his younger brother had done, cognizant of where the spines were and weren't. With a few controlled snaps of his wrist, he chopped off the tips of all the dorsal spines, Marley's bundled-up dreadlocks barely budging with each beat. "Only the tip of the spine has venom," he said with calm confidence, as if he were holding a class.

The scales around the spear's entry point had been shaken off by the impact. He scratched the rest of them off with the side of the knife. And with them went most of the striped coloring, revealing paper-white skin. For the lionfish, beauty is only scale deep.

I mentioned to him that we only saw one other lionfish during our outing. "Before, they were everywhere," Marley said.

And then, the sobering dissection. "I always check the stomach when cleaning," he said. It is a task that many lionfish hunters regularly perform, to better understand the abilities of the enemy. He carefully sliced open the greyish, oblong pouch inside the lionfish's belly, revealing an equally grey 2-inch fish. Its scales and fins had already been digested, making identification of the species difficult. But the destructive power of the lionfish was unmistakable. Proportionally, it was as if an adult human had just swallowed a football in one gulp.

*****

Therese Castillo, better known in Hopkins as Miss Therese, was picking limes from a tree in her backyard when I presented her with the plastic bag. The day before, my wife and I had met her ("Look for the woman selling bread at the bus stop," we'd been told) and we had arranged to have her prepare a dinner of Garifuna dishes at her house in Hopkins, where she often cooks for guests and tourists.

My beach shoes sinking into the sand of her yard, I opened the bag to show her the lionfish, now filleted, along with a couple spiny lobsters and a hogfish that Noel had caught on the day's fishing trip. She had prepared spiny lobster and hogfish countless times, but never lionfish.

She had a way of commanding the moment by just placing her hands on her plump hips and arching her back. I had no choice but to wait to see how she'd react. She looked into the bag. Her brows jumped up and she gasped. Then the gasp became a smile, as if I were giving her a present. I asked, "What are you going to do with the lionfish?"

"I'm gonna fry it."

*****

Two hours later, my wife and I were seated at a card table, covered by a tablecloth with a rustic flower pattern, on the sand of Miss Therese's yard, about 100 feet from the gentle Caribbean surf — gentle thanks to the protection offered by the reef. At age 57, Miss Therese was proud to tell us that one of her sons, taking after her, was a chef in a restaurant near San Pedro. "I paid for my children's education with this table," she said, pulling up a chair at our request. I never knew that such a memorable romantic ambience could blossom from a card table and a fluorescent bulb dangling from a nearby tree branch.

"People think Garifuna food is just rice and beans," Castillo said as we all tore into the bounty in front of us: broiled spiny lobster tails; fried hogfish; fried lionfish; plantain dumplings in a thick coconut broth (a sweet, starchy traditional Garifuna dish); a pitcher of limeade; and a stew of gibnut, also known as paca, a cat-sized rodent prized in Central and South America for its porky flavor.

The lionfish was dwarfed by the hogfish on the plate, but both had a similarly light yet luxurious meatiness. The Garifuna had arrived to what is now Belize more than 200 years ago, long before the lionfish appeared, but Castillo had no difficulty figuring out how to cook up the newcomer. Without its venomous plumage, the lionfish is just another fillet to fry. I would not be surprised if fried lionfish ends up joining the canon of Garifuna cuisine.

*****

The next day, when we arrived in Placencia, a peninsular town about an hour's drive south of Hopkins, we found that outside a jewelry and gift store, a local artist had produced his own interpretation of the lionfish threat: a painting of a sultry, reclining mermaid with the fiery stripes and graceful fins of a lionfish. Dangerous beauty indeed.

We turned down the town's sidewalk, a sort of raised boardwalk of concrete and wood planks running above the sand, and passed the faded clapboard of pole houses, until we found the Placencia Producer's Cooperative. "BIGGEST LIONFISH: 744g; SMALLEST LIONFISH: 10g" read the handwritten poster, on the wall of the cooperative's store, listing the results of Placencia's 2013 Lionfish Tournament. A total of 599 lionfish had been speared by three competing teams of scuba divers in the nearby reef.

To encourage the spearing of lionfish while simultaneously offering local fishermen a worthwhile alternative to targeting overfished species such as grouper, the cooperative began a project to purchase and process lionfish. The fillets would be shipped to restaurants in North America and beyond. The cooperative had just acquired its FDA license to proceed.

I met Justino Mendez, the operations manager, inside his windowless but heavily air-conditioned office, and asked him how the project was progressing. And where could I find the cooperative's lionfish served in the States?

"We're at the promotion stage," he told me. Unfortunately, no restaurants had served their fillets yet, because the cooperative was still getting the word out to fishermen and importers/exporters alike. If Mendez has his way, though, in a few months' time, we will be seeing blackened lionfish, lionfish pot pies or lionfish sashimi on the menus of New York City, Chicago and London restaurants. Lionfish is already being served in several South Florida restaurants, since Florida has already begun its own culinary campaign against the invader.

Can eating the problem make it go away? According to information gathered by the National Oceanic and Atmospheric Administration, scientists familiar with the life cycle of the lionfish are doubtful. The jaws of humans will never completely eradicate the species from the Caribbean and Western Atlantic. The lionfish is here to stay.

So we might as well enjoy it, guilt-free. Flambéed in a piña colada sauce. Or ceviched, as I'd had at the Hour Bar, a busy waterfront café in Belize City. Or perhaps you should enjoy it the way that seems to suit any fish in the sea: fried.

Darrin DuFord is arguably the only connoisseur of both wine and slow-cooked jungle rodent. He is the author of "Is There a Hole in the Boat? Tales of Travel in Panama

Without a Car," silver medalist in the 2007 Lowell Thomas Travel Journalism Awards. He has written food and travel pieces for the San Francisco Chronicle, BBC Travel, Roads & Kingdoms, Gastronomica and Perceptive Travel.

ERIN BYRNE

HEALING HEIGHTS OF MACHU PICCHU
Peru

Then up the ladder of the earth I climbed
through the barbed jungle's thickets
until I reached you, Macchu Picchu.
—*Pablo Neruda, "The Heights of Macchu Picchu"*

"And now we will go up to this temple of the Inca," said Eddy, our crinkly-eyed guide. Quick and agile as lizards, my husband and two sons scuttled after him, their backpacks swinging, and disappeared around a corner.

My foot refused to move.

The trail, about 8 inches wide, was carved into a cliff high in the Andes Mountains. This was a place called Pisac, where the air is dry and thin and chases the heartbeat like a wild animal. My foot reached out invisible tentacles and clung to the stone step from which it was supposed to spring. I tugged; it stayed.

I might have known. I am the woman who, 12 years earlier in the wilds of Anaheim, CA, gingerly crept up the steps and wobbled across the rope bridge to ascend the steep incline of Tarzan's Treehouse — and froze in this same way. Kellan and Brendan's eyes were astonished rings as I, their mother, rapidly returned to solid ground.

It is I who suffered shaking spasms and cursed aloud when they leaned over the guardrail at Yellowstone Canyon, climbed slippery rocks under Yellowstone Waterfall, or dangled from the railing of Yellowstone Bridge to spot a jumping fish below.

I am the one who clung to the front rail of the chairlift with one hand while the other twisted the collar of Kellan's ski jacket for a firmer grip; who waited impatiently below among roving pickpockets while Brendan climbed the steps of the Eiffel Tower; who flatly refused my husband's invitation to join him for a whirl on the London Eye.

I am pretty sure I have acrophobia, an irrational fear of heights. Psychologists advise against avoidance, advocating slow exposure or even virtual reality, which has shown "significant progress when patients are confronted with real height circumstances." Exaggeration, they say, is common in acrophobes. Eighteen inches, for example, could shrink to 8.

I'd planned this trip to celebrate both a high school and a college graduation and to honor John's dream that began when he was 4 and saw the cover of National Geographic. I had been consumed with planning a flawless itinerary (Cusco, the Sacred Valley and Machu Picchu, then Brazil) and worrying about the symptoms of altitude sickness or contaminated water or my terror of spiders. It had somehow slipped my mind that I was horrified of heights.

Until the first hour of the first day of the first week up there on the precipice in Pisac when in my marked distress, I suddenly recalled a line from Pablo Neruda's poem, "The Heights of Macchu Picchu: "Point out the rock on which you stumbled."

Neruda, the Nobel Prize-winning Chilean poet, was suffering from his own malaise in 1943. He'd been isolated and cynical, sunk deep in a hollow-eyed depression, sulking about man's ominous dwindling each day like a black cup, sea of death. He paced the world alone, dying his own self-obsessed death, losing his poet's heart, until he reached a dead end.

Then he traveled to Machu Picchu.

"The Heights of Macchu Picchu" which he wrote two years later, inexplicably adding an extra "c," reveals how he surrendered to the stone citadel in the sky: He first opened himself up and sensed it with every antenna in his body, then he imagined the Inca people living, laboring, loving, and finally he praised the place like a lover with two-phrase bursts of pure adoration.

We would be there in a few days. Meanwhile on our tour through the Sacred Valley of the Urubamba River, dry-mouthed and wild-eyed, I hugged walls of granite, willing myself not to look down and tensed in terror as I rounded every corner. My body in a state of high alert, I was wearing myself out with worry and missing most of what Eddy was teaching us about the sacred sites of the Inca. The thought that this was the only chance I'd have to be in Peru for a very long time, possibly forever, made me fume with frustration.

Obviously it was far too late for slow exposure or simulated heights. I don't do drugs, but in quest of any kind of relief I cast off my motherly mantle and began to slurp cup after cup of coca tea — I didn't know it would take roughly 200 times as many leaves to even begin to resemble the drug. My nerves were too frayed for the invigorating effects of coca tea, anyway.

Finally, desperate, I decided to emulate Neruda's process: be open, sense, imagine, praise. I did not expect to receive a promise in return.

We visited places where the agile Inca hauled, shaped and molded rhinoceros-size boulders weighing as much as 100 metric tons. We scaled more inclines at the Sacred Temple of the Sun at Ollantaytambo and explored the stone circle of terraces at Moray, which formed a kind of amphitheater. We crossed walkways that felt to me like balance beams above the salt pools of Maras. All the while, Eddy alerted us to dozens of incredible enigmas:

"There is the quarry over there (pointing across a ravine to another mountain 2 ½ miles away), and we don't know how the Inca got the rocks up here to make the temple. The wheel was sacred to them and they would not have used it for transport.

"They had enough grain in the storage structures built in the side of that mountain to last five years (pointing to a series of alcoves built directly into the side of another mountain).

"These blocks have no mortar between them; the Inca engineers designed them to fit together with room to move. During many major earthquakes here in Peru, the colonial and modern structures collapsed and these remained.

"The Inca people cut the rock and shaped it this precisely [Eddy stuck the corner of a credit card in a tiny crevice to show how tightly the blocks fit, a bit like Legos] and the only materials they had were gold, silver, copper and bronze. That's all. How did they cut into the stone?" His booming laugh echoed across the expanse of space as he slapped a rock. "We don't know!"

These sacred ruins presented so many vivid images and unanswerable questions that I found myself consumed with the mysteries, following Eddy and my three lizards eagerly, if awkwardly, scampering up skyward staircases, only occasionally clutching at someone's belt loop or shirt collar. By the time we boarded the train to Machu Picchu, the fear, although still there, had begun to fade into the background.

We climbed off the train and boarded a bus that careened up to the place that had dwarfed Neruda's human condition.

We faced Huayna, "Young Peak"" in Quechua, the ancient language of the Inca. It looked like the sleeping back of a wooly green alpaca. Off in the distance clouds sauntered past snowy peaks against a backdrop of deep royal blue. We stood on Machu, "Old Peak," a gigantic fortress of geometric precision. The stones were stacked in the outlines of a city, and grass and wild orchids grew on terraces that had once held corn, peppers, squash, potatoes and lupine.

This green-blue kingdom in the air seemed to exist in a new, elevated dimension I'd never visited before. There were people scurrying around everywhere: Men strained as they carried heavy loads on their backs, mothers ushered children away from a group of llamas, a few elderly women leaned on their walking sticks, laughing. The very second Eddy mentioned details, these scenes of the Inca appeared in my mind and the atmosphere of the place (that essence that can never be shown in photographs or described in mere words) emerged for me.

"The roofs were once thatched, and the cooking fire would have been here in the center." A woman gazed out the trapezoidal window, cradling a bowl holding ingredients for a meal, yellow peppers, potatoes, cuy (guinea pig).

"Families lived and worked in community." Children laughed and shouted as they jumped down steps, splashing in the stone-carved canals that carried water from mountain springs.

"Careful planning included architects, engineers and astronomers." Men huddled together around a torch, talking and gesturing with wide sweeps of their bare arms.

"Here is the Intihuatana, the Hitching Post of the Sun." A crowd gathered in the chill of the morning. As the sun lit in a bright triangle upon the exact spot on which their eyes were riveted, a collective gasp hissed, followed by the whoosh of an exhale.

"There was a fountain here, and here, and here." The soothing sound of tumbling water trickled and licked at the stone in a steady rhythm that never slowed or stopped.

While my being was busy being in this place, I could feel the remnants of my acrophobia float off like feathers: I stepped without measuring the distance to the edges, and I quit calculating cliffs. It was odd that it happened so fast, but I didn't even notice; I climbed without resistance. In my state of reverie, I rose above the confines of my body and traveled beyond the jagged peaks into the sky. The higher, the better.

That was when that thing I had previously thought of as the mystique of travel — all that stuns, shakes and shrinks the self — transformed itself into a promise that if we open our senses and imaginations to a place, we can be flung far back in time, or sent spinning beyond our weak selves, or even sometimes healed of that which we hold onto that holds us back.

It was a mystery to me how it happened, but Machu Picchu seemed to cure my fear of heights in the same way it had changed Neruda.

Then we traveled to Brazil.

Dusk was descending at Posada Bromelias, a cluster of bungalows high on a hill in Mata Atlântica, the Atlantic Forest. I peered down the path into a deep, green universe burgeoning with sound and movement: choruses of chirps and croaks, buzzing and bizzing, glops and glugs and distant splashes and crashes, rustling, crunching, spinning and swooping. The last threads of daylight revealed darting movements on vibrating feathered fronds and dark wings flapping and stretching. Through the fading light I could make out trunks rising up and vines hanging down.

The air was thick and moist with the heady scent of orchids and some kind of sweetness that slowed my blood and turned it to syrup. I imagined thousands of eyes in the form of dots, rings, slits, some heavily lidded and reptilian, some miniscule and beady, peering out at us from the foliage; and monkeys swinging from their tails on branches high above; and intricate, lacy webs that would glisten in the moonlight.

I felt the cold approach of another fear extending its eight letters toward the edge of my consciousness: a r a c h n i d.

But it didn't creep in; it stayed stuck in an insignificant misty fog outside of importance while I exalted in the overwhelming rhythm of this astonishing orchestra's grand performance.

My foot did not hesitate as it stepped into the jungle.

Erin Byrne writes travel essays, short stories, poems and screenplays. Her work has won numerous awards, including three 2014 Travelers' Tales Solas Awards, and 2013 and 2012 Grand Prize silver and bronze for Travel Story of the Year. Her work appears in a wide variety of publications, including Points North Atlanta, World Hum, Travelers' Tales Best Travel Writing and Burning the Midnight Oil anthologies, and Vestoj, The Journal of Sartorial Matters.

Byrne also wrote The Storykeeper, an Accolade Award-winning film about occupied Paris. She is an occasional guest instructor at Shakespeare and Company Bookstore in Paris, and is co-editor of an anthology of writings from the bookstore, Vignettes & Postcards From Paris, winner of 10 international awards. She is working on Wings From Victory, a collection of her stories about France; a novel, The Storykeeper of Paris; and the film Siesta, to be filmed in Spain in 2014. Details can be found at e-byrne.com.

MARIUSZ STANKIEWICZ

FEAR IN SRINAGAR
Kashmir

At the end of my backpacking trip, I found myself way up in the northern reaches of India, a far distance away from the heat, pollution and dizzying crowds I first encountered two months before in Mumbai.

Despite all the warnings by my parents, a few fellow backpackers and some newspaper headlines suggesting against any sort of traveling to Kashmir, I disregarded all efforts to change my course and decided to make Srinagar an essential stop on my scrambled, city-hopping itinerary. My goal was to explore Ladakh first, the "Land of Gompas" and reverent worshippers of Buddhism, before heading west to the Muslim-dominated city located in Indian-administered Kashmir.

As Srinagar sits amid the eight-thousanders, its winters are often snowed in, halting any sort of transport for months though making it perfect for skiing, particularly in Gulmarg, a heavily-militarized ski resort town with more soldiers stationed than visiting ski buffs. It lies 35 miles from Srinagar and is only a short trekking distance from the Line of Control, the Indo-Pakistan border. Given the kind of traveler I am, this was neither the weather nor the kind of "personnel" I wanted to encounter. Despite being Canadian, snow and I are as incompatible as fire is with ice, and considering Srinagar's current state of affairs, I simply had to prime myself for the inevitability of guns, fatigues, barbwires and sandbags.

During the summer, while most of the Indian subcontinent is feeling the monsoon rains, Srinagar keeps its cool and receives a most reasonable summer exodus from the lower and hotter regions. Its peaks remain snow-capped yet bring out the region's alpine scenery quite nicely, a temperate wonderland amid an "abode of snow," what the Himalayas is often referred to. Dal Lake, the "Jewel in the Crown of Kashmir," boasts rare wildlife and even shimmers by a combination of a golden sun and modest wakes widening aft by Shikaras, Kashmiri "Gondolas." Kashmir's beauty is such that the Mughal Emperor Jahangir's erstwhile praise cannot be any more fevered in his exclamation: "If there is a paradise on earth, it is this, it is this, it is this!"

But this romantic designation has lost its credibility since India's independence movement. Led by the father of a nation, Mahatma Gandhi, the fight for autonomy eventually pushed British India into relinquishing control and to partition the country on grounds of religious demographics. Not too long after, Lord Mountbatten, the governor general of India, signed off on 335 years of British Colonization. Frontier wars broke out between the newly formed Dominion of Pakistan and the Union of India. Separatist uprisings, insurgency and general political strife created, ironically, an atmosphere of hell on earth rather than Jahangir's envisioned paradise.

This unrest has been synonymous with Kashmir since the mid-20th century. The 1994 kidnappings and deaths of four American tourists by Kashmiri separatists exacerbated tourism even more. Two months before my visit, another tragedy struck, this time in the Pakistani-controlled regions of Kashmir. Ten international climbers at Nanga Parbat's 13,000-foot base camp were rounded up and shot to death by gunmen dressed in police uniforms yelling out "Taliban! Al Qaeda! Surrender!"

Visitors were once advised against any non-essential travel to Srinagar — and to some extent still are by several foreign governments — yet a period of relative calm (notwithstanding isolated incidents or minor skirmishes) has given way to a revival of tourism. A recent headline from The Guardian made the effort to assure that things are improving: "Kashmir is back on the tourist map."

However, there was no way of ignoring warnings from travel posts and forum messages conveying what the word on the street was: There is an ongoing conflict here, come visit at your own risk, we are not responsible for anybody exposed to the risk of violence.

While staring up into the ceilings of the various types of accommodation I'd come across — thatched hut in Hampi; mildewy concrete in Goa; a mosquito net in Pondicherry —the question kept popping up in my head: Should I go to Srinagar or should Leh be my last northern destination? Should I put myself at risk for the sake of my stubborn curiosity, for my insatiable appetite to "feel it on my skin," as my Italian friend, Luca, says, rather than to read about it in the papers? Most important was the question: If something were to happen and I were to survive, would I be able to deal with the trauma?

After spending some time in Ladakh, I finally stood up to my own doubts and took a bus to Kashmir via the Leh-Srinagar Highway (NH1D). The highway spans 422 kilometers (262 miles) throughout Jammu and Kashmir and took approximately 13 hours to get through, half of which I sat curled up into myself hoping I would overcome the most frightful bus ride I'd ever been on in my life.

A few thousand feet up high near Fotu La Pass, on a road that resembled more of a crumbling ledge, our van came face to face with a bus. There was no way for both to pass at that stretch of the road — there simply was no room, somebody had to reverse down the mountain but that, too, was an absurd alternative.

We drove toward each other entering, what appeared to be, the death dance of a vehicular kind, an unmatched pas de deux of rubber tires, steel and frayed rope holding up bumpers. It would commence the moment both transport vehicles would meet in a merciful display of martyrdom, as though they knew fairly well that any one of us could be falling off the cliff within the time it took to pray. Our driver would inch closer, then the bus would match the distance just as slow, and this would go on until both appeared like two mechanical dolphins about to nub each other. Then, to my glorious surprise, we would gradually, synchronously, slide our exteriors passed each other to the right at two or three inches; the bus would also appear to be sidling two or three inches from the cliff's edge at a turtle's pace.

My face was up against the window the whole time. I felt beads of sweat hovering above my brow. Some passengers were watching the whole spectacle nervously; others were sleeping, exhausted from fear altogether. I saw both drivers not only give each other anxious salutes when their windows aligned, but a mutual farewell in the event that the "dance" would end with a tragic byline printed in every newspaper in India. And a photo — a photo showing a mangled wad of steel akin to a cat's ball of yarn. As frightening as the moment was, I try to recall it using humor as the best way to minimize the reality of death that could have fallen upon us.

A few hours later we were traveling in the black of night and it was no less dangerous than making that 5,000-meter-high pass during the day. The van's headlights were weak and a thick fog blanketed the narrow road making visibility beyond three meters impossible. The driver, to my shock, was driving only a bit more cautious even though the vehicle's suspension seemed to be losing its battle against the dirt roads and dangerous hairpins. He was mumbling to himself the whole night, too. I never did figure out what he was saying. I assumed he was reciting words from some scripture, perhaps praying to some multi-armed deity or big-bellied Buddha, hoping that our transport would lead us to our earthly destination and not to the heavenly one.

He kept the window open to make sure the cold would keep him awake — and to pretty much freeze those inside who didn't have a blanket. Unfortunately, I was one of them. I packed lightly, allowing more weight for my camera equipment. Luckily, I was able to curl up under the blanket of a fellow female traveler from France who took an interest in me, the highlight of this nightmarish transit.

At 2 or 3 a.m. we were so high up in the mountains that when I looked down from my window I saw the night sky. The night sky? But how? How could I have spotted stars down below through grey clouds when they should be up above our heads? Did something happen without my knowledge and we were already en route to the Kingdom of Heaven?

After blinking my bleary eyes feverishly, I soon discovered that the "stars" were distant villages with faint road lighting reminiscent of some diffuse galaxy. That is how high up we were, so high that we were floating beyond the clouds in the cosmos and seeing our reflection in a big body of water on earth.

We rode into Srinagar at approximately 5 a.m. I hadn't slept a wink. Dawn was starting to break, revealing a layer of fog atop Dal Lake. The other passengers were asleep, yet the driver's freakish last leg to get into town for *salat* (prayer) quickly jolted them out of their sleep. The city center was quite somber, like a ghost town, for lack of a better word. It was empty except for a few worshipers walking along the promenade heading toward a place of worship. Indeed, the sight was like ghosts walking atop misty water.

I heard the *adhan* coming from some minaret's crown recited by the temple's muezzin. This call to prayer is a statement of faith for Muslims the world over, but the moment I heard it I realized how much I desperately needed to sleep off the night's suspense. I couldn't gather any energy to head out and to explore just yet.

No sooner had we arrived than I opened up my friend's Facebok wall and read that her jeep traveling near Srinagar was attacked by men armed with sticks and guns. I was shocked. She described them jumping on the car and hitting it. When they tried to open the door to force the driver out, the driver managed to break away, run back in and lock it. They did manage to pull the passenger out of his seat and beat him — but he, too, quickly escaped and got back inside. My friend, Beatrice, whom I had met way back in Manali, was the only foreign passenger. Luckily, they managed to escape but it was a brush with death she never expected.

It was that moment I went back to my houseboat and contemplated leaving. After much thinking and discussing the situation with the houseboat owner, I decided to stay. I would not give up on Kashmir just yet.

My houseboat had an elaborately-carved wooden balcony reminiscent of an Oriental hand fan, and it served as the perfect backdrop to my reading and writing. I took down notes about what had happened to Beatrice. I didn't know if she arrived at where she was going, but I even worried heading back to that same Internet café to open up my e-mail and Facebook page.

At times I stared out at the mirror-like waters of Dal Lake thinking about what she had gone through. Occasionally, I had the privilege of being visited by a Kingfisher, India's national animal. If I was really lucky, I'd see it dive off the houseboat's banister into the water. This preying on pan fish was happening no more than two meters from where I kicked my feet up to relax, though I couldn't really relax, as I needed assurance that Beatrice was well and safe.

I went to bed early that night to get my mind off things. I decided on an early excursion the next morning to see a unique 200-year-old tradition.

I woke up at 5:30 a.m. to see my rented shikara bobbing at the houseboat's entrance. It came complete with a smoking driver who, despite being able to speak English, remained mute the whole excursion and focused on pulling on his cigarettes casually while I was taking photos of the lake, landscapes and people washing their clothes in the water.

No sooner did I get changed than we set off for the floating market, a hidden jewel not many travelers know about. Winding through swampy backwaters full of water trees, bushes and river cabbage, we finally came upon a lagoon on which a flotilla of longboats was crunched up together so close that one man could have walked — using the boats as steps — all the way to the other side. Men in dhotis and collared shirts were either standing or kneeling in their boats, adeptly maneuvering their boats around, balancing their produce on medieval scales, counting money or chatting with other men. They were all trading (or selling to the few tourists I encountered on the most lavish-looking shikaras) flowers, saffron, tomatoes, red-tinted cucumbers and spiny bitter gourds at wholesale prices.

We got back around 7 a.m. to have breakfast and, immediately after eating, I quickly got into my next activity, which was to climb Shankaracharya Hill. Right when I was about to get into the shikara to be taxied to the Boulevard Road, my host called me back and handed me a big stick. "What is this for?" I asked. "Bears haven't been spotted in a while, but there are leopards, tigers and panthers in the hills." I was left speechless. "Leopards?" I asked. He nodded his head. I grabbed the stick feeling there was nothing else I could do. This, too, wasn't something that would force me to give up on Kashmir.

The trek was a winding 5.5 kilometers (3.4 miles) up toward the Shiva temple built in 200 B.C. It was an outing surprisingly peaceful and calming and free of predatory animals or unscrupulous macaque monkeys ready to pilfer your pockets for whatever kind of edible. The time spent atop the hill was quite rewarding. Seeing the city down below from up high dissolved my worries even more — yet, still, in the back of my mind, a few of them kept me highly alert. I walked back down without seeing any suspicious bushes rustling, any fanged felines or unusual animal calls. Feeling relieved, I took a bus to Hazratbal Shrine.

Built in the 17th century on the banks of Dal Lake across the Nishat Bagh, Hazratbal Shrine possesses a courtyard full of massive Chinar trees, a marbled dome (though currently under construction wearing a helmet of bamboo scaffolding), and is even said to house the Moi-e-Muqaddas, a relic consisting of a lock of Prophet Muhammad's beard. I exploited a perfect photo op of the shrine's courtyard with the lake and mountains in the background, as well as the shrine's entrance gates pullulating with worshipers and flocks of pigeons, a spot ideal for photographers to experiment with moving subjects incorporated with still ones. The ride back to the houseboats from the shrine was an eventful 25 kilometers (15.5 miles) with many other photo ops along the way including the Shalimar Gardens, the centerpiece of Mughal horticulture studied in landscape architecture classes throughout the world.

I felt a bit better when I arrived at the Boulevard, as its familiar sight assuaged any of the discomfort I previously had. It was virtually absent of large crowds or any other kind of metropolis-borne anxiety, unless you consider the touts who brazenly market *shikara* rides, aimless *tuk-tuk* commutes or quietly whisper "you want good Kashmiri hash?" The honking of car horns I noticed was significantly less than in Delhi or Mumbai. Then again, the next day brought with it an *Eid al-Fitr* celebration where youngsters quickly broke their Ramadan fasting and took to speeding their scooters and activating their horns madly for no reason but to anger the locals.

I took a bus to the Old Town and explored the back alleyways until I came upon the sacred Hari Parbat temple. I heard the *adhan* again, a half-song, half-vocal melody, calling upon Muslims to pray. I felt something mysterious yet empowering happening within me, something which instantly filled me with inspiration and allowed me to be at peace with myself and with the world around me.

Some random thoughts entered my head. I began to think how important it is to "create" your own calling in the world and not "find" or "wait" for it to happen. I began to realize how everybody needs to leave some kind of footprint behind in the world, to make a statement of their own, be it religious or not. This statement for me was of a professional kind involving the pursuit of information, social change and global communication through travel writing and journalism.

"The voice of that recording masks the pain and suffering of Kashmiris," said a man who had approached me asking if I was a journalist (I was carrying two DSLR cameras which certainly gave way to such an assumption). I was invited to sit down on the grass under a tree. In casual repose, we discussed the state of his nation. He mentioned that he was deeply concerned about the future of his people. He blamed it on how the world viewed his land and its disgruntled citizens; infighting and the Kashmiri problem. Tourism, as a result, had been on the decline as separatist fighting was sporadic yet never-ending. I became interested in his words, which galvanized me to write about my experiences, to tell the world about this region. I wanted to know more, to find resolve in full awareness of this crisis, and to see how it could be overcome. Regardless of all the good or bad thus far, there was still passion in my heart and an undying curiosity in my eyes.

The meeting had a strong effect on me, but I was suddenly left confused the moment we were interrupted by a young man in his early 20s. He came out of the shrine and asked if I wanted to go with him to photograph his friends who were about to incite a riot. A riot? I didn't want to ask. My journalistic instincts were activated, but something deep down inside felt wrong in tagging along with him, as though my camera's presence would make them do things they normally wouldn't.

This feeling of unease was soon justified the moment he knelt down and pulled out his phone. He played a video for me which I could only watch, in complete horror, for about three seconds. He claimed that the man in the video was an Indian soldier stationed near the Line of Control and that many more should be beheaded for violating their human rights and stopping them in their fight for freedom.

At that moment I was visibly nervous. I interpreted this as a warning, yet again, a warning among a set of earlier warnings telling me I shouldn't have come. I was scared and could only think about those Americans who were kidnapped and killed; the newspaper headlines; letting down my family. I agitatedly yet meekly thanked the people who were starting to gather around me and quickly left, walking back down toward the city. I looked back and saw one man starting to walk fast behind me with angry eyes, as though he were offended that I had departed without any kinder words or appreciation for sitting down on sacred temple grounds. That was when I bolted and never looked back.

I caught a bus back to the touristy Boulevard and sat on the edge looking out at the water. I wondered what my remaining days in Kashmir were going to be like, if all those warnings would persist being only warnings and nothing more. I hoped I wouldn't become a minor detail buried in one of the many facts justifying travel warnings in general, in India or even in the entire world and in those few dangerous, enter-at-your-own-risk areas.

Regardless of what had happened I stayed for the last six days of my trip. Regardless of what will happen there would be nothing in this world except death itself that would stop me from experiencing even that single, illuminating and compassionate gesture from humanity while searching for myself, even if it would come at the cost of dozens of bad situations or fearful moments. I feel that travelers need to crush any kind of fear through the act of experiencing and moving around the globe, through seeing and opening up to the world. There is nothing else but to confront fear, cope with it and move beyond it. It is a fact of life that either prevents you from becoming a better person or succeeds in you being mentally boxed in and fearful of any hoot or howl in a dark jungle.

In the end, the blue Kashmiri sky seemed to be the only thing I couldn't achieve, yet after backpacking throughout India for two months, I was sure to have had plenty of it already.

Mariusz Stankiewicz is a Canadian freelance travel journalist based in South Korea. He also worked as an English instructor at Busan University of Foreign Studies in South Korea. He has published travel and lifestyle pieces in various magazines and newspapers, including Verge, Barcelona Metropolitan, In Travel, Travel Maga-

zine UK and The Province/Vancouver Sun. He has worked on photography projects in Thailand and assisted in photo assignments in Mongolia and China for the German Press. His photos and travel blog can be found at mariuszstankiewicz.com.

PETER MANDEL

WALKS ON THE WILD SIDE
Uganda

Uganda is a forest of words. Its placards grow as tall as pine trees, perched up at the pinnacle of poles, swinging from wires, hanging out in front of stores. I squint, and shade my eyes (since this is noon in Africa). I try to understand.

Ugandan signs are bold along its roads, clear and bright as its sun. "Full Cream Milk Powder," says one. "Grow Faster, Grow Stronger." "Drink Fresh Water," urges another. And then: "This Land is Not for Sale."

"Is that about pressures from the West?" I say to my guide. "About all of the YouTube hype over the Kony film?"

My guide simply stares. "The sign means this," he replies. "The owner does not wish to sell."

Before I came here, Uganda was a land I thought I knew. The Invisible Children video showing abuse by Joseph Kony's rebel army was all over the Internet.

Still, there are the signs. Signs of a place where daily life is distant from the wars and issues and debate. Distant, even, from its years of British rule and from former dictator Idi Amin. Landlocked in East Africa, Uganda's population is more than 85 percent rural.

Outside of big cities like Entebbe and the capital, Kampala, I find that almost no one I talk to knows about the Kony video. I am American, and all I get are smiles. Sometimes a little dip of the head. An outstretched hand.

"Come to see our animals," says a man I talk to at a store along a country road. "We are different here than Kenya, Tanzania. You can get up close. You will see them. And, of course, they will see you."

*****

At my first stop outside Kampala, there are still more messages on signs. Here at Ziwa Rhino Sanctuary, some of these signs show rhino shapes and say: "Beware." I'll try. I'm with a group that's trying to get as near as we can to Uganda's newest rhino — re-introduced here after their disappearance in the area in the early-1980s.

According to our guide, Opio Raymond, some of the sanctuary rhinos come from Kenya. Some are from Disney's Animal Kingdom Theme Park. One is named Obama.

"NEVER move in front of the guide," we read. "ALWAYS move in single file.

Then comes the part in bold:

"Should the rhinos show any signs of annoyance, you should STAND BEHIND A LARGE TREE IF AVAILABLE. OR MOVE NEAR A TREE AND BE READY TO CLIMB."

I take a look around. The trees I can see look a lot like saplings. Thin and scrawny. They look like trees that rhinos might eat for a snack.

"These are white rhinos, though they may look gray," says Raymond, as he leads us up to a fence. We pass through a gate and form our line. I have never walked in a file as organized as ours. Raymond seems pleased.

He scans our clothing and spots someone's crimson shirt. "The rhino does not see well," he says. "But when they see pure red, they do not like it."

What should I do? asks the tourist with the shirt. Raymond just shrugs.

We are told that there are anti-poaching rangers around who carry rifles. They won't be of use to us. It's lunchtime for sanctuary staff. And Raymond is not armed.

When Raymond stops in his tracks and crouches, our rhino conga line crouches too. There are whispers. What are we seeing? We are seeing spoor.

"The poop for the rhino," our guide explains. Raymond picks it up in his hand.

"Nice," he says. "Take a look."

Shortly we are studying a print — three rhino toes — when Raymond spots her. Behind some bushes is a female rhino, Bella. Dinosaur eyes. Prehistoric horn.

Raymond flaps his hand for us to approach. Our line strings out, snaps back. We're there.

From what we can see from maybe 50 feet, through branches, Bella isn't alone. There's something gray and squat that's crowding in, insistently pushing, just below her belly. "Baby," says Raymond simply. "Time for nurse."

All is peaceful. Rhino mother and child. Reverent sounds of cameras.

Then Bella moves.

There is a scuffle. It is on our side of the bush. No one wants to be obvious, but we are scanning around. "MOVE NEAR A TREE," we think. "BE READY TO CLIMB."

Aside from bushes, there is grass, and some kind of weed. Maybe we could climb up Opio Raymond.

There is a thump. Is this a sign of annoyance? The start of a charge?

Bella's horn is lowered, an ominous pose.

A man in our group who may be 60, possibly more, has told us matter-of-factly that the battery in his pacemaker is dead.

I look at Bella, and at the man. Their eyes are locked.

The rest of us are staring, staring. Bella turns a hoof. She scuffs.

No one runs. We have heard the story of a photographer who fled. A rhino named Hasani hooked his camera with his horn. Then Hasani trapped him under his legs when the man fell down.

No one runs.

And, after a second, Bella's movement is finished.

Opio Raymond smirks. Some of us seem sheepish. The man with the pacemaker looks pale.

It's nursing time again. Maybe a nap. Our mother rhino gives out an animal sigh.

She is done with hauling her body into a lazy stretch. She is exhausted from all of the efforts of lying back down.

*****

Later, in the Uganda bush, I book a room at a lodge called Chobe. It is a set of terraces, decks and plate-glass windows looking out at rapids along the Nile.

"Do not ignore our view," says the porter who is dragging my bag over pebbles and mud. He shades his eyes like an explorer. His hand sweeps up and across.

"Fifth best scenery in Africa," he says.

I find out later it's the workout room at the hotel that has been cited for its panorama view. But, when I see my tent that's near the banks of the river, I realize: I do not need a treadmill.

This is the Nile, I think.

I start exploring at once, picking my way down grassy, reedy banks. Ahead is a group of warthogs, bent at their forelegs, pulling grass — chuff, chuff, chuff — too focused to care. My flip-flops frighten bright blue lizards. A mongoose pops its head up and disappears.

There are ripples in the muddy water. Ripples made from rocks? Not rocks. This is the Nile.

I see some sets of eyes. Two here. Two over here. A bubble pops. There is an extended, resonant sound, something like a bassoon.

"Hippos," says the porter, blandly, leaving me with my key. "When darkness arrives they come to sleep under the tent porch."

I check this out. In fact, my tent has a floor, and furniture and mosquito netting looped around its bedposts. I peer through a floor crack: no animals now.

But while I am watching, one of the river wallowers hauls itself up on land. Dripping on the grass, it begins a yawn. I root for my guidebook: "An open mouth," I read, "may be a sign of aggression. Hippos are among the continent's most deadly animals. They've bitten humans in half."

This image is in my mind for days. Behind every boulder I imagine hippos, crouching stealthily, waiting to emerge.

One afternoon I am with a tour group that is tucking pants in socks, spraying for tse-tses, and gearing up for a walk. We are in Kyambura Gorge in Queen Elizabeth

National Park. The goal of our hike is to see chimpanzees. We are ready, binoculars at hand.

Our guide is named Jimmy. "Just Jimmy," he says. "That is all."

Jimmy gives us pointers near a muddy trail that will lead us deep into the gorge. He and his assistant, Henry, look like infantrymen in dark green uniforms and boots. Henry has an automatic rifle "just for keeping safe."

"If need be," he says, "we shoot at the skin of the animal and make it sleep forever. We do not kill."

"A Ugandan Buddhist," somebody whispers. I am not reassured. We begin our slide down the path. My sneakers scoop up leaves and some kind of beetle, several pebbles, and a sharp-edged stick. These are flushed out when the trail we're following turns into a gurgling stream.

With so many trees overhead, the gorge is as dim as a museum. And just as silent. Shade is changing everything, as if a candle has replaced the sun. Is that a giant mushroom? Is that a pumpkin? Real and imaginary merge.

After hours of criss-crossing Kyambura, Jimmy points out a knuckle print from a chimp who has, at some point in time, passed by. There is a colobus monkey who shows us his tail and disappears. And then a chunk of Pterygota fruit that, according to Henry, "a chimp has used as a cup."

It has started to rain. We stop again and again to scrutinize the canopy. Not one branch swing. Not one shape.

But somehow I am tingling. The hair on my arms is on end. Is this some kind of sickness? Jungle paranoia? Maybe I am ill.

Chimpanzees are up there, I am sure. They are staying disciplined and quiet. Probably following our group. Keeping just out of view.

I tell no one about this worry. I begin to perspire.

At the bottom of the gorge, I know why I've have been tightly alert.

It is hippos who have been watching us. Not any monkey.

Africa's most dangerous animal. They are scanning us, eyes and nostrils visible, as we come down to their lair, as we step out on a fallen tree trunk to cross the chocolate river at the bottom of the gorge.

They are watching us as we scramble and slip, scramble and grip at filigree branches, back to light and air.

They are watching, and blowing baritone bubbles, and making plans.

*****

Back at the lodge, it is nighttime and we are driven in golf carts down to the Nile, back to our furnished tents.

We talk of Africa in the dark. We stare at reeds and river.

There is a slice of moon. It picks up shapes spread out along the bank. Strong shapes. Low slung. One silhouette is close to someone's tent porch.

A woman in the back speaks up. "Hippos," she says. "Do they ever chase?"

"Yes, they do, ma'am," says the driver, braking so he can talk. "Sometimes they do."

"What would happen if they caught you?"

"It is bad," responds the driver. He is trying to restart the motor. "They bump you. Then they..."

The engine has stalled. Crickets call.

There is the sound of the bassoon.

Everyone but the driver reacts. We leap out and scramble the rest of the way to porches, slipping on gravel, kicking flashlights and keys. We make it. Lamps snap on.

During the night I keep on waking from a Nile-long dream. Deep-voiced porters are calling. I am wearing crimson, and reading roadside signs.

Porters are calling. They are calling me to the gym, the gym with a view.

But there is an orchestra out there. A section of woodwinds. Brass.

I'll sleep forever, I think.

I will not die.

Peter Mandel is an author of books for children including the new "Zoo Ah-Choooo" (Holiday House),

"Jackhammer Sam" (Macmillan) and "Bun, Onion, Burger" (Simon & Schuster). A regular travel contributor to The Washington Post and The Boston Globe, he has written for Harper's, The Wall Street Journal, International Herald Tribune and Los Angeles Times. His articles have won several Lowell Thomas awards from the Society of American Travel Writers. He lives in Providence, RI. See petermandel.net.

MIM SWARTZ

LAST TRIP TO VENICE
Italy

I took my husband to Venice for his birthday for the last time. He stayed, and now Tom Carney is a resident of La Serinissima, "the Most Serene," as the one-time independent republic was known.

That Monday afternoon, Tom's ashes were dispersed in the *Laguna di Venezia* outside the city we both loved.

Venice was our favorite place in the world, a spot where we would try to visit whenever we were within 1,000 miles because we could never get enough of it. We had been there about 10 times, and loved soaking up the atmosphere in off-the-tourist-track neighborhoods. Venice is unlike any other city — it's not only beautiful, with imposing centuries-old palazzos that line the Grand Canal, but also peaceful, because there are no automobiles. Boats and feet are the main modes of getting around.

Years before, Tom and I had talked casually off and on about his desire to have his ashes scattered in the waters of our beloved Venice. The discussion became more relevant when he was in the hospital about a month before his death. He suggested an alternative place in Colorado, "If you can't make it to Venice."

After he died, I thought, why can't I? So I started making plans. In truth, I probably did it as much for me as for him. I wanted to visit Venice with Tom one last time.

But it wasn't easy. A burial – at sea or on land – in a foreign country comes with a slew of rules and regulations.

It would have been easier, perhaps, had Tom specified a scattering at sea in Venice in his will. It took me almost seven frustrating months — although final approval came, Italian-style, just days before I departed. And it was not cheap: Not including travel necessities (airfare, hotel, local transportation, food, drinks and glass-bead jewelry – oh, the jewelry!) it cost about $3,400 for paperwork, fees and funeral boats.

I now feel that I know more about "Death in Venice" than the novel's author, Thomas Mann.

And the whole time I was jumping through hoops planning the trip, I could hear Tom's voice: "This is idiotic nonsense, Mim. Forget it. Don't go to all that trouble."

But, I'm not a newspaper reporter for nothing. Tenacity is our trademark. I never have given up easily. And I'm glad I persevered this time, too.

*****

People probably have been throwing urns with ashes into Venetian waters for centuries. However, I knew that Tom, a lawyer, would want me to do it legally.

I Googled "Venice and cremation" and up popped stories from two London newspapers. They said that under a law that city officials passed in 2010, cremains were for the first time allowed to be scattered from certain spots in Venice's waters.

I decided six months before his birthday to start with the vice consulate of Italy in Denver, but after making a phone call, I learned that the office wasn't functioning. I needed to go through the Consulate General of Italy in Chicago, which handles Colorado. The consul general told me that all the forms I needed were on the consulate website. But those forms weren't pertinent, only dealing with bodies and caskets and shipping, not cremains being carried.

I called Chicago again, and this time got voice mail. No one called me back.

In searching the Internet, another organization surfaced: the International Scattering Society. Its website said the group "was founded to educate and to assist families with scattering cremated remains worldwide ...."

The laws and regulations vary in different countries, and our staff are experts in handling international scattering requests." It added that the society "can help you with local contacts, acquiring permission or obtaining a permit."

Great! This was going to be easy, I thought, especially since the website showed Venice on a map of locations, with a photo of a gondola filled with people on the Grand Canal. I called the phone number in Lee's Summit, Mo.

But the woman who answered the phone said the society did not have contacts in Venice, and didn't know how to go about arranging a burial at sea. So much for that website.

"This is idiotic nonsense," I heard Tom saying.

I was getting worried. So I asked a Denver friend who was born in Italy and has cousins in Sicily — a sea away physically and mentally from Venice — if she could ask her relatives to make some phone calls. What was I thinking?

That, I did know, was idiotic nonsense.

I called another friend in San Francisco who helps feral and stray cats in Italy (Tom and I had gone on a "Cats and Culture" tour she sponsored in Italy in 2006) and asked if she could contact one of her Venetian friends to see what exactly was required. Her contact eventually sent me pertinent computer links through the *Comune di Venezia* (City of Venice) website — with information that, of course, was all in Italian.

Meanwhile, I had found another website. This one was for the Italian Institute in Denver, which offers Italian language classes, translates documents and helps plan travel in Italy. I met with founder and CEO Maria Chiacchio, who said she could help. I gave her a down payment of $250 and left her to her own to deal with her fellow countrymen.

Over the next several months, Chiacchio was in frequent contact with the Italian Consulate in Chicago and the City of Venice's Mortuary Police office, which is in charge of issuing a required mortuary passport. But the consulate even had difficulty getting responses from Venice: The process of dispersing ashes in the waters of Venice is new for the city, and presents complications, especially if you're not an Italian citizen. I was beginning to wonder if the 10 friends and family members who planned to be in Venice for Tom (and me) on his birthday Oct. 7 would be making a trip for naught.

Administrative assistant Cristiana Ninci with the Chicago consulate suggested that I hire a funeral home in Venice to help expedite the process. Weeks later, when Chiacchio contacted one, things started to happen. The funeral home was able to do some necessary legwork in Venice.

It was mid-September.

At one point, Chiacchio's e-mails weren't even being answered by the funeral home. It turned out the owner forgot to pay the bill for his Web domain and his e-mail was cut off.

And, when Chiacchio still wasn't hearing back from Venice, she e-mailed the mayor, asking why no one from the Mortuary Police was responding ("I added the mayor's address to see if they would wake up!").

The mayor never responded personally, but the next day, Chiacchio heard from the city. E-mails started flying fast and furiously during the next couple of days. I chuckled at all the exclamation points and the word URGENTE! in the subject lines.

And while I couldn't read Italian, I knew things were close to coming to a head when I could make out the request for "€ 363,38 *inerente la dispersione ceneri di non residenti nel territorio del commune*," the fee (about $550) for dispersing ashes of a non-resident.

Chiacchio tried to keep me calm through all the drama, assuring me "it's just the way Italy works," and adding that, politically and economically, things are very difficult in Italy right now.

Finally, a week before I was to leave for Venice, Chiacchio sent the e-mail I had been waiting for. "We got it!!!! They are sending the mortuary passport!"

The day after it came, a bill arrived for the remaining balance of Chiaccho's services and reimbursements, bringing her total fee to $2,595.

*****

A TSA agent called me aside when I went through the security line Oct. 4 at Denver International Airport.

He asked if there were ashes in my carry-on bag and wanted to do a swab test. He said cremains show up in the X-ray machine as "bad stuff" — they apparently have the same consistency as explosives. I was tempted to tell him that, well, Tom did sometimes have an explosive personality, but I knew better. Never make jokes with airport security officials.

No one asked for the mortuary passport when my friend Barbara and I arrived the next morning at Marco Polo Airport in Venice, although the Chicago Consulate had said immigration would. I e-mailed Chiacchio in Denver to tell her the irony. "Of course, right?" she responded.

And, despite all the documents that Chiacchio had sent to Chicago with notary seals, *apostilles* (seals authenticating documents to be used in a foreign country) and other official verifications, the funeral home informed me that I would need to go to the Mortuary Police office in Venice Monday morning — Tom's birthday and the day of the planned ceremony — to sign more papers.

A man from the funeral home arrived at my hotel at 8:30 a.m. and we walked in pounding rain to the city office. Three women pored over the file with worried looks, speaking fast Italian. Finally, they asked for the mortuary passport. Aha! All was not in vain. Then I had to sign three copies of a form confirming that the ashes had been dispersed in the Venetian Lagoon, although that wouldn't be occurring for another six hours or so. I asked what would happen to all the papers, and was told they will remain in the files in Venice. As far as I could tell, I was helping keep at least three people in jobs.

By 2 p.m. when the two funeral boats arrived, the rain had stopped and clouds cleared, allowing blue sky to peek through. Our entourage of 10 motored out into the lagoon near the island of St. Michele, the home of Venice's cemetery (with celebrity residents Ezra Pound and Igor Stravinsky). Church bells chimed. We raised plastic Champagne glasses filled with Italian sparkling wine in a toast to Tom while his daughter, Diane, recited Alfred Lord Tennyson's "Crossing the Bar," which we had found while searching the Internet for something appropriate for the ceremony. It begins:

"Sunset and evening star,
And one clear call for me!
And may there be no moaning of the bar,
When I put out to sea."

I took a deep breath, leaned over the side of the funeral boat and gently dropped the papier-mache box into the lagoon. Tears flowed (along with the bubbly Prosecco) as the biodegradable "Aqua Journey earthurn" with Tom's ashes gracefully skimmed the water for a couple of minutes, then sank. Brenda, one of the women in our group, poured some Prosecco into the water "for Tom."

Afterward, we had a mini-Irish wake at the venerated Harry's Bar – one of Ernest Hemingway's and Tom Carney's favorite haunts — then dinner later at my hotel restaurant, where there were more toasts and tears.

It was the perfect ending to an emotion-filled day.

*****

On our last night in Venice, there was one more thing I had to do before saying ciao. Barbara and I walked to the unequaled Piazza San Marco, which earlier in the day had been flooded with *aqua alta* (high water), but now was dry. There is not a more beautiful place to people-watch and listen to *musica* from the small rival orchestras playing outside three rival historic cafés. You can stand all night and enjoy the sounds for free, but if you sit you pay a supplement of €6 each, about $8.35. Tom and I didn't mind paying for music, and were always amused by the white-coated waiters who never batted an eyelash over the menu — they are expert at acting like there's nothing outrageous at all about the prices.

Barbara and I settled at a table in front of Caffe Quadri, which dates to 1638. We ordered a cappuccino and a glass of red wine, along with two ice cream sundaes, one strawberry and the other chocolate. The bill, including *musica*, came to €63.50 — almost $90.

That, indeed, is idiotic nonsense. But it's Venice, the mesmerizing, magical island city built on mudflats with an improbable existence. It is difficult to depart. You do so only because you leave your heart and know you will return — idiotic nonsense or not.

Arrivederci, mio amato marito. Goodbye, my beloved husband. *Ci vediamo.*

Mim Swartz, an award-winning former travel editor of the Rocky Mountain News in Denver and The Denver Post, lives in Golden, CO.

AARON PAULSON

THE DAY THE EARTH MOVED
Japan

Bright Tokyo sunlight spills like holiday wine into the classroom. The fine weather makes it even harder for the students to stay in their chairs on this Friday afternoon before spring break. Never mind other distractions, like the roar of an airplane close overhead or the rumbling of earth-moving equipment as it passes close by the school.

The students try their best. Sixteen heads bend over laptops, gamely putting final touches on term papers. Finish this, they know, and it's smooth sailing into two weeks of vacation.

But that earth-moving equipment just keeps getting closer and louder, coming down the road, then for some reason pulling into the parking lot at the front entrance of the school.

Bizarrely, it moves into the school itself, comes down the hallway, through the closed door, the noise and vibration impossible to ignore as it comes right inside the classroom with us, and I think we all realize at the same time this is no earth-moving equipment at all but a temblor, an earthquake. A big one.

Maybe even The Big One?

Tokyo, a world-class city of 36 million, lives in a collective state of denial. Along with Tehran and Mexico City, Tokyo is a city of "high seismic risk." Bill McGuire, a prominent volcanologist and professor at University College London, has pronounced Tokyo "the city waiting to die" because of its susceptibility to natural disasters. Japan, after all, has a 4,000-meter (13,423-foot) volcano on the outskirts of its capital, which last erupted a mere 300 years ago. In the 1923 Great Kanto Earthquake, more than 100,000 people died in the initial quake and subsequent blaze sparked by cooking fires. Maybe this is why Tokyoites work so hard, putting in long hours at the office and on commuter trains packed tight as sushi rolls. They want to avoid thinking about what might happen the next time a big disaster does hit the city.

In fact, big ones strike with such regularity that a legend has sprung up about a giant catfish asleep in Tokyo Bay. From time to time it tosses and turns, and shakes the ground under the city. The last time the great fish awakened was 91 years ago. Another wake-up is overdue.

This legend of the giant catfish was exactly the new way of thinking I wanted when I left for a three-year stint overseas, to see what I would make of the great big world, and what it would make of me; to be inspired, to gather new material and to raise a grubstake for further adventures.

Now, some 13 years later, I surprise myself at how easily I have put aside dreams for the comfort of stability.

The school doesn't feel so solid at the moment, however. Unlike all the previous quakes that strike us on a regular basis, this one doesn't stop shaking after a few anxious moments. Instead, the tremor comes to life, becomes more animated. The giant fish struggles awake.

A pause, a matter of a heartbeat or two, just enough time for everyone to let out a nervous laugh. Then a shudder, and the shaking starts again, stronger than before, like two waves collapsing on top of each other, becoming more than the sum of their parts. And we're not just rocking back and forth the way we usually do; the building also jumps in place, as though being walloped from above and below.

Something to write home about, I think to myself.

The shaking ratchets up yet another level of intensity and the ceiling-mounted monitor swings wildly over my head, out of control, threatening to crash down. I don't need any more prompting when the principal orders everyone to take cover.

Suddenly, a teacher's worst nightmare, I have lost control of my classroom. I no longer know what's happening around me. I can't see my students, who are folded up like origami under their own — suddenly rather flimsy-looking — desks. Then something smashes to the floor, and someone screams.

"You're OK!" I yell from my own huddled position. "Stay down."

It occurs to me, absurdly, that this classroom I've worked in for almost nine years now, where I've taught hundreds of students, is turning against me. I feel like I've just been mugged in my own neighborhood: the familiar made strange, even dangerous.

Meanwhile, the walls flex like the sides of a ship in a stormy sea.

Another absurd thought: Perhaps the whole school will break free from its foundation and sail away, and take us with it.

Then, just as the quake wound up, it starts to wind down.

I look out from my hiding place, expecting the ruins of a devastated building. The reality, however, is not nearly so terrible. Japan has made strides in earthquake-proof building design, and it seems to have some success. Cupboards have sprung open, spewing orange and green Halloween decorations. Nekko, a ceramic cat that does duty as class mascot — and unwitting character in stories and classroom demonstrations — has smashed to pieces in front of the whiteboard. However, the walls and ceiling, and the windows and doors remain intact.

A big one, then, but not The Big One. A shake-up, certainly, a rattle of the nerves, and the rest of the day — probably the whole weekend — will be jazzed with adrenaline. But the school has remained anchored to its foundation. It seems that the giant catfish under Tokyo Bay just stretched its fins.

Then the PA crackles back to life: More tremors imminent; evacuate the school immediately.

On the way out, some students have the presence of mind to grab jackets and smart phones. I think about bringing the can of green tea I'd been drinking during class, but why bother? The seriousness of the situation still hasn't registered. We'll be out of the building an hour tops, I figure. Then school will let out, and I'll go back to my classroom and putter around until quitting time. Back to business as usual.

Uniformed students parade into the space between a water-filtration plant and some farmers' fields still winter-barren. At first they dutifully line up in neat rows behind their teachers like so many gray and black ducklings. Excitement levels run high, however, and soon the lines bend and break. We group into ever-changing knots, sharing stories. From the air, we must look like pictographic characters written in the dusty playing field, spelling out fear and excitement about what might happen next.

I feel more alert than I can remember, no longer daydreaming about my upcoming trip to Taiwan but firmly rooted in the present, my winter-dulled senses sharp again.

One of my students has her phone out, and looks worried. "Any luck?" I ask.

"There's no signal!" she wails, betrayed, staring helplessly at the little screen.

"Try again in a bit," I reassure her. "Everyone's probably trying to call right now. The system's just busy is all."

Not for the first time, I question whether being "the last person in Japan without a cellphone" is really such a good idea. My wife, let's call her R., works across the city — all of Tokyo lies between her and our little suburban apartment. I have no way of contacting her to find out if she's all right.

But no one is getting through anyway. I picture this great, congested megalopolis faulted into small groups of people: tribal-sized units clustered around parks and train stations, office buildings and department stores. What will happen, I wonder, if we are on our own, cut off from civilization like the boys in next semester's novel, "Lord of the Flies?"

And something else is amiss, though it takes me a moment to figure out what.

"Is it just me, or are we still moving?" I ask the other teachers near me.

"That's just vertigo," the PE teacher says.

Other details start to pop into focus: A huge military transport airplane circles low and slow overhead. Crows and flocks of songbirds also hang in the air, afraid to land, as if they know something dangerous waits below.

"That's a bad sign," the art teacher says.

Meanwhile, the students have fallen silent, and stare at something behind us. A thick black rubber water pipe, which normally hangs between two of the school buildings, swings now like a jump rope from near-constant aftershocks. So my muscle memory and over-active imagination don't deceive me after all. The ground still moves beneath us, and this earthquake still has some life left in it.

To make matters worse, clouds the color of dirty rice water move in low from the west, and the temperature drops quickly. Most of our students wear only their school uniforms: a light blazer and slacks or a skirt. Fortunately, the school has emergency supplies cached in two metal storage sheds. A group of teachers unpacks silver reflective sheets and brown felt blankets and passes them over the fence to waiting students. These will help with the cold, but we've still got problems if those clouds turn to rain.

An executive decision gets made: We will take shelter in the school gymnasium.

An empty school is a ghost ship. Shadows inhabit the place. They walk the hallways, sit in the desks, drink at the water fountains, and are at their lockers when they should be in class. More than once I've come in on the weekend to catch up on work, only to leave early, my tasks incomplete, rather than spend an afternoon alone in a place usually so full of life, now barren, empty.

We teachers watch through the night. In the wee hours of the morning, I pick my way through bodies spread around the gym – a cavernous, hollow building in the dark, lit only by the red emergency beacons above the fire hose and heart defibrillator in their red cabinets, and the blue light of faces illuminated by laptop monitors. It's just as well. What kind of rest could I expect, what kinds of dreams would I have, if I tried to sleep after seeing that stream of images over the Internet? The same scenes over and over again: of an oil refinery burning volcano red and running like lava in the night; of the tsunami wave surging over seawalls, sweeping away bridges and cars and trucks, tossing fishing boats and trucks alike into second-floor apartments, tearing through houses made of matchsticks, of papier-mâché, a churning, roiling mass of angry, bestial water that travels inland for miles over the rice paddies and the industrial lots of the coastal plains.

Still, here in our school gym, we have heat, light, running water, and even the Internet. After we adjust to the almost constant tremors, the basketball nets waving in an invisible breeze, we feel safe, maybe even a little dismissive of the whole business.

So instead of sleeping, I walk through the brightly lit elementary school classrooms. It's way past 2 a.m., but little pockets of activity spring up in unlikely places. In one room a teacher video Skypes with a reporter half a world away. In a stairwell, a gang of 12th grade boys eats bowls of spicy instant noodles. In the office, the staff is up all night, checking updates online and drinking coffee.

Back in the gym, some students manage to sleep in nests of blankets and school blazers. Others stare mesmerized at their computer screens.

I make a little nest for myself and try to get some rest, but the tremors feel stronger this close to the ground, and overhead the stage lights and movie screen still rock ominously. Even so, the rush that's kept me going since the afternoon has worn off, and I fall into a few hours' exhausted sleep.

By morning, our numbers have thinned considerably. Despite the hazards of crossing the city, a steady trickle of parents has managed to reach the school and pick up their kids. We bus the remaining students, teachers and staff members to the closest working train station.

Out of the gym and away from the school, it seems as if nothing has happened. Just another bright, beautiful spring morning in Tokyo. The trains run almost on time, and the local headed into the city has plenty of empty seats. Still, as we move sedately through quiet residential neighborhoods, I can't tell if it's my nerves, the normal shunting of the train cars back and forth, or yet another tremor which makes the train car shake so.

A bare 15 minutes later, I arrive at my home station. Already the events of the night before seem, to my exhausted, sleep-deprived, over-stimulated mind, like a hallucination, like a piece of puppet theater or a kabuki play. Despite power outages in some parts of the city, the local KFC is still open, and I pick up a chicken wrap and corn salad on the walk home. In our little bento-box apartment, R. greets me, safe and sound. One small bookcase has toppled over; otherwise everything appears normal. I wolf down my food, then pass out on the futon.

The days and weeks that follow make a surreal landscape of earthquake and tsunami and nuclear meltdown crises; of rolling blackouts here in Tokyo and refugees and blizzard-covered ruins up north; of heroic first responders and nuclear plant employees; of conspiracy theories on the Internet and media images of white-masked "survivors" moving zombie-like through bleak, apocalyptic landscapes. Rumors spread virally across the Internet and Twittersphere of entire towns disappearing, and passenger-laden ferries and Shinkansen bullet trains being swept out to sea. And for the rest of us, the unfolding specter of a nuclear meltdown at the crippled and possibly leaking Fukushima Daiichi power station. Basics like rice, bread and bottled water disappear from store shelves. Along the normally busy road I walk each day to the station, long lines of cars, their drivers patient, ghost-silent, wait at the gas pumps – noone wants to be caught with empty tanks if the order comes to evacuate the city.

Radiation "hot spots" bloom in the shadow of the wind from Fukushima, even all the way out here, in western Tokyo.

I still suffer from vertigo, still feel the ground slip away from under my feet. Once, I have to grab R. to stop from falling down the stairs. My emotions remain volatile. I can discuss my own situation calmly and rationally with my wife, family and friends, but go weepy when I think of the "Tohoku 50" power plant workers ruining their lives with radiation to protect the rest of us, or the bleak video of a young woman who stayed at her post, warning others to high ground even as the fatal tsunami wave swept in. Running errands downtown, I watch a policewoman put herself between fast-moving traffic and a stranded pedestrian. I want to thank her for her bravery, for her simple, everyday act of self-sacrifice. But I don't have the words to explain myself. Instead, I give her a big smile as I pass. In congested, anonymous Tokyo, she nearly chokes on her whistle in surprise.

Back home, is that yet another magnitude 7-plus tremor rollicking the overhead light, or just the work crew jackhammering in the next lot? I move pairs of strong shoes and a "go bag" of energy bars, sports drink, warm clothes, a flashlight from bedroom to living room and back again as we navigate our days.

Still, some silver does line this dark cloud over Japan. I walk home in a blacked-out city, a ruddy sunset reflecting in the darkened windows of shops and houses, and in the faces of other commuters. I wouldn't normally notice such details, jacked into to my iTouch and thinking of my day at work, but this crisis is another country's worth of new experiences, and I am alive again to first impressions.

Then, boarding a train one afternoon, I notice a young couple sitting across from me with a box of Krispy Kreme doughnuts in their lap, and I know: We're going to be OK.

No doubt about it: life in Japan has changed, even as far from the disaster zone as Tokyo. And the giant fish at the bottom of Tokyo Bay has awakened, and may shake its tail again at any time. Still, we learn and adapt. My heart no longer skips a beat every time I check the news online. Once again I start to think beyond the next half hour, and rebuild a daily routine derailed since the earthquake.

*****

When R. and I married in the spring of 2010 on a mountaintop in the wilds of western Tokyo, I made a promise to the local *tengu*, the mythic warrior birdmen who protect Japan's cedar forests and mountains: Watch out for us in this life, I told them, and, when the time comes, we'll join you in looking out for others. Looks like we owe them one.

Aaron Paulson is an American-born, Canadian-raised teacher, writer and photographer who's made another home in Tokyo since 1998. His work has been featured in such national and international venues as Salon, World Hum, Transitions Abroad, Tokyo Journal, Kyoto Journal, and most recently The New Idealist. You can catch him virtually at home on his website, aaronpaulson.com.

MAGGIE COOPER

SAILING DOWN UNDER
Australia

Here there be monsters.

So read the legend on maps of old, written by those brave (or foolish) enough to set sail for the unknown in tiny ships, searching for fame and fortune.

Those sailors of yesteryear relied not on satellites, radar, depth sounders, carbon fiber and Kevlar but on their wits, the stars, the wind and the benevolence of the gods. They inscribed "Here there be monsters" on the boundaries of the known world to describe the potential horrors awaiting them just beyond the horizon when they really didn't know if they might or might not sail over the edge of the ocean.

My personal monsters are – in no particular order – growing old, not growing old, change, vegetating and running out of good stories. There are a few contradictions in that list; being a longtime adrenaline junkie, the "growing old" and "vegetating" entries have highest priority. To paraphrase Neil Young's iconic song of the '70s, "Into the Black," I'd rather burn out than rust. I've long believed that there are worse things than being dead, having watched my beloved mother take way too long to die from the curse of Alzheimer's disease.

So, like others of my generation – the Baby Boomers – I've always followed the credo of carpe diem and live with the consequences. Therefore, I (a tail-ender Baby Boomer clinging tooth and nail to the last of middle age) seized the day well and truly when I was invited to sail alongside my newish partner Bruce Priestley from Tasmania to Queensland, from the bottom of the east coast of Australia almost to the top and back in the latter half of last year on his cruising yacht, the Brenda J.

Neither of us is inexperienced; I learned to sail in my 20s and Bruce has formal marine qualifications as part of his job as technical scuba instructor and proprietor of a dive shop. But long-distance cruising was a new thing for me; plus, the last time I was on a yacht with a man – a fiancé, no less – cruising the Whitsunday Islands inside the world-famous Great Barrier Reef back in the '90s, we were trapped below deck for three days in a mini-cyclone and never spoke to each other again. Before this trip a good friend advised me that a cruising boat gets a foot shorter every day you're on it ... so, would our relationship survive?

Preparation took many months; there was work to complete (my food, travel and pop-culture columns for an Australian newspaper depend on a reliable Internet connection for filing stories and photographs on time and a kitchen much larger than the galley onboard the Brenda J), provisioning, house- and pet-sitters to be sourced and interviewed and, most importantly, there was a steep learning curve ahead for me to acquire the necessary knowledge to be a safe and reliable sailing companion who could pull my weight.

That meant picking up the workings of a whole grab bag of technology introduced since my early sailing days. Radar, Emergency Position-Indicating Radio Beacons (EPIRBs), reading charts, navigation light identification, GPS, radio protocol and navigation software – to say nothing of fighting mild seasickness while draining a pot of boiling pasta, propped in a corner of a galley pitching around in a 9-foot swell – all these skills needed to be mastered.

Mastered they were – although the weather conspired against us and we ran out of time in the latter stage of our preparations. The shakedown cruises we planned prior to setting off were canceled, leaving me to learn on the job while sailing across the big-boogeyman Bass Strait (one of the most feared and dangerous stretches of water in the world) for the first time. Not ideal. Plus the Brenda J is a good 20 feet longer than the last yacht I sailed; extra hull length and width translates to a much larger sail area. I really didn't know if I would be strong enough to handle the helm.

I discovered a bar isn't necessarily a place to relax with a drink, but the often-dangerous entrance to a river. I also learned by trial and error how to do the washing up in a sink smaller than a sheet of computer paper, with less than three inches of lukewarm water in the bottom, holding the plug down with one hand to prevent the water pressure under the hull of the yacht popping it out every time we fell off the top of a wave while all the time grabbing a conveniently placed rail so I didn't end up on my butt.

The Brenda J is a 30-year-old fiberglass Roberts-design ketch with a central cockpit, built for cruising. The vessel is comfortable and roomy; Bruce stands 6 feet 8 inches tall in his bare feet and isn't fond of bending double, so the headroom below deck was an important consideration for him when he purchased the Brenda J three years ago. But its size, while reassuring at sea, provided logistical problems when making landfall; a lot of marinas aren't geared to cope with a vessel of that size and some waterways are too shallow for safe passage in a boat that draws almost 2 meters (almost 7 feet). We ran aground (gently) a couple of times, luckily on a soft bottom of sand or mud.

Once, while crossing the notoriously tricky bar at the entrance to the Clarence River at Yamba on the mid-north coast of New South Wales, we noticed a large number of people lined up on the shore, many armed with cameras. While drinking in the local pub several nights later, after safely entering the anchorage, we discovered while chatting to a local that they had all turned out to film us as we crossed the bar; many visiting sailors and boaties, unfamiliar with the conditions, come to grief. Word spreads quickly when a strange vessel is spotted off the coast and they all grab their gear and run for the foreshores for a night of cheap entertainment.

There were a few moments when I could have turned into the two-legged panic beast. Bass Strait, which we crossed on Days One, Two and Three of the voyage, is around 150 miles wide and sailors not infrequently die crossing the water between the island state of Tasmania and the mainland of Australia.

Partway across on the first night our steering broke in heavy seas and strong winds where Banks Strait empties its volume into Bass Strait; Banks is a narrow passage between Tasmania and the Furneaux island group. The full force of the ocean, goaded by the strong winds, causes the water to bank up many feet above sea level as the sea is forced through the gap. Bruce is a competent mechanic (among other attributes) and he calmly dismantled the components of the steering mechanism, fixing it and restoring order in less than an hour.

Later in the trip we ran into foul weather and endured several nights of being thrown about violently like we were in a washing machine. One memorable evening heading from Sydney to Jervis Bay we had green water (translation – a very large wave) crash over the bow and into the cockpit.

But right from the start, I realized that a panicky woman would be of absolutely no use to anyone and would, in fact, turn an unpleasant experience into a potentially fatal one. So I endured the cold, the wet, the fear and, once, being thrown out of the watch bunk in my sleep, clearing the lip as gracefully as an Olympic high jumper and hitting the deck with full force (but thankfully without breaking any bones).

The yacht carries most modern conveniences; still, our priority when we reached shore every few days was a decent hot shower, a cheap'n'cheerful meal at the local lawn bowling club (always the best value) and a chilled beverage that involved alcohol (unlike those long-ago sailors with their daily shot of rum, for safety's sake we avoided the booze while at sea).

Cleansing one's self at sea is dodgy at best; our shower facilities involved a hand-held hose with an outlet a little larger than a quarter, and limited hot water, so it's a case of wet down, turn water off, soap pits and bits, turn water on, rinse off. All to be accomplished while being pitched about, naked and slippery, in less than two minutes. And as for more intimate functions ... at the risk of being vulgar, the marine toilet (called the head) was the focus of much angst for me; it had a nasty habit of backing up at critical moments and twice overflowed when it was a really, really bad time for it to do so – I can't emphasize enough how bad a time it was. At one stage we were contemplating having to use a stainless steel bucket with, ahem, "manual emptying;" luckily

Bruce's humble status of Handyman was elevated to that of My Hero when he managed to fix yet another problem.

Chief danger on the three-month odyssey was the very real possibility of colliding with a migrating whale. The population of the eastern Australian humpback fell as low as several hundred during the mid-1960s at the height of the whaling industry, but they're like cockroaches now – huge, powerful (but mercifully gentle) 36-ton cockroaches. At any given time, several thousand move up or down the east coast; they travel during the birthing season so it was common to see several females traveling behind the pod, gently escorting a newborn calf between them.

We narrowly avoided ramming several and had one juvenile almost land in our cockpit off Coffs Harbour while we were under sail (and therefore silent); it breached not 6 feet off the starboard rail and possibly suffered as big a fright as we did – although I doubt it. The impressive upper-body display was followed by a leisurely flick of a giant fluke that showered us with spray; had we been inclined we could have reached out and laid our hands on its smooth, glistening body.

On another occasion, ironically off the former whaling town of Eden on the south coast of New South Wales, I was catching up on some sleep, lying in the sun on the aft deck, when I was rudely awakened by a loud exhalation and I was enveloped by a fine spray with a strong fishy odor. I sat up abruptly to find the blowhole and curved back of a humpback arching gently out of the water about two feet off the starboard rail; the leviathan had come up to take a breath and had spouted all over me.

Whales also provided the greatest frustration of the trip (apart from the wind being from the wrong direction for that time of year). We were, at times, literally surrounded by the gentle monsters of the deep – and yet failed to capture one decent happy snap of their constant aerial displays, despite having two competent photographers and a raft of state-of-the-art digital camera equipment on board. It became a running joke between the two of us; the second a pod would make its presence known I would bolt for my camera; my return topside would be the signal for them to disappear for an hour or more.

We sailed from Bicheno in Tasmania to Brisbane in southern Queensland and back – falling considerably short of our intended destination of Cairns in far-north Queensland, thanks to the failure of the expected southerlies and work-related deadlines that meant we had a non-negotiable date for our return.

We made it back safely with not a single cross word between us; a stronger bond (built on sheer trust); an enormous sense of achievement; and 2,545 miles under the keel.

Will we do it again?

Most certainly; this year's trip to Kimbe – on the island of New Britain in Papua New Guinea – is in the planning stages as we speak.

Old age? Phooey.

Maggie Cooper is a freelance food, travel and pop-culture writer whose columns appear weekly in an Australian newspaper. She lives in several locations surrounded by the spectacular natural beauty of Tasmania, Australia's island state.

JAMES MICHAEL DORSEY

OF NOMADS AND WHALES
Mali

From the back of a camel the Sahara seemed endless; an infinite sea of low rolling dunes baked by a swirling sun that would be at home in a Van Gogh painting.

For one month I had been immersed in Berber Tuareg culture, traveling through Mali as one of the famed "Blue Men" on the trans-Saharan caravan routes they had operated for more than 2,000 years. We carried no maps, GPS or satellite phones, navigating only by landmarks, intuition and the inbred sense of direction that is part of nomadic DNA.

They were fierce desert warriors, straight out of central casting, lords of the desert, the bane of any bandits who crossed their path. And they had allowed me to enter their world.

Tuaregs are called the "Blue Men" usually because of the indigo robes and turbans, (called a tagelmust) they wear, but the real reason stems from the fact that they use the ink of sea urchins to create this luminous color, and after time it permeates the pores of their skin, rendering them permanently blue. They range across several countries in North Africa, and call the desert by a different name in each place. Sahara is a term used only by westerners.

When a friend put me in touch with a Tuareg nobleman who lived near Timbuktu, he was taken aback by my request to live and travel among them, but readily agreed, as intrigued by me as I was of him. How would these nomadic Muslims, a unique sect of Islam in which only the men cover their faces, react to me, a white, western Christian, entering their world?

My thoughts immediately recalled the journey of Sir Richard Burton, who, disguised as a wandering beggar, became the first white outsider to enter Mecca as a pilgrim in 1852. Had he been discovered, he would have forfeited his life. While I had no illusions of my trip being anywhere near as dangerous as that of Sir Richard, I knew it was still pushing the envelope a bit. I am, after all, an infidel.

My Tuareg contact, Halis, was tall and dignified with an air of self-confidence that filled the room. His blue robes were trimmed with gold, denoting his standing within the Tuareg hierarchy, and he wore the silver medallion around his neck the Berbers refer to as their passport, a talisman that wards off evil while announcing the travelers' native village. His words put me at ease regarding my acceptance or rejection by his fellow tribesmen, informing me they would consider my attire to be a compliment.

His cousin, Mahmoud, would drive us into the desert where we would meet our mounts, and I found him to be a friendly but somewhat feral man whose scarred face betrayed a hard life. In the days ahead I learned that Mahmoud slept with one eye open and his knife half drawn at the hint of any intrusion, deciding that in the desert these were admirable qualities. In their combined company I felt secure because when a Tuareg gives his word, he will die for it.

We drove from Timbuktu to the crumbling former foreign legion outpost of Arawan, about 100 miles north, now a watering stop for caravans hauling salt from the northern mines near Tademmi, south to Timbuktu. Stepping out of the Land Rover in my blue robes, I was welcomed by a young Tuareg, who simply walked over to me and, with a slight bow, handed me the rein to a camel.

That evening I sat around a small fire, wrapped in blue and surrounded by desert warriors, eating seared goat and rice with our fingers in a scene unchanged since the time of Christ. Except for Halis, they spoke their native Tamasheq and a few spoke French, while I spoke neither and did not care. They were men of few words and I needed none. I had entered a society I had thought was closed to me, and I was absorbed in the moment.

The next morning we left by camel to complete a wide arcing circle of the southern Sahara, visiting numerous nomad camps along the way. By the end of the first day my camel had already bitten me on the leg and showered me with his urine, but I learned quickly how to control him and was soon mounting and dismounting as though born to it. At each new nomad camp I was immediately served sweet tea, as custom demands, and taken to see the head man, and always was treated as a Tuareg without reservation.

I expected at all times to be inundated with questions about the outside world, especially about the United States, but realized these people live such an isolated existence that their world and curiosity extended no further than the immediate needs of the day. Where I came from, and who I was, was irrelevant. The words America and airplane had no meaning for them. I was just an outsider from many days' ride away, but now I was one of the tribe, helping with daily chores, tending to camels and listening to ancient tales around the occasional evening camp fire. I slept the sleep of the dead, rolled in my robes, under the desert stars.

The contrast with my own society was overwhelming. While those of us who live in the Western world spend most of our waking hours in front of one sort of electronic screen or another, these people found joy in the tiniest, most intimate moments, particularly in relating funny stories or retelling oral histories. It was a simplistic life, free of stress and full of laughter, a daily search for the spiritual and a way of life unchanged in 2,000 years. By the end of the second day, I was already questioning my own material values.

Though they were primarily Muslims, they had no reservations about having this Christian infidel in their midst. To them I was just another traveler, and the law of the desert required them to offer me hospitality, which they did freely. I found this to be more Christian-like than many who simply professed the faith without applying right actions.

It struck me that I never saw any of them openly praying as I had expected, and when I finally got the nerve to approach the subject with Halis, he patted his heart and said "God lives within here. I pray all day long." When I told him that was my own approach to religion, he just smiled lightly and said, "I know."

On our final day approaching the outskirts of Timbuktu, Halis looked every inch the Tuareg nobleman on his amber-colored camel, with myself in the middle, and Mahmoud, hand on his dagger hilt, scanning for trouble.

I spotted a man standing on a wall, dressed head to toe as an ad for REI. The two cameras around his neck identified him as a tourist, and he was raising his long lens directly toward us. Without thinking I held up my hand and called loudly, "*Cadou! Cadou!*" meaning, "Give me money if you want my photograph." It was common enough among poor local people to ask for a few coins in such a situation, but why I did it so reflexively I cannot say, other than I was caught up in the moment.

Halis immediately picked up on what I was doing and began to laugh softly under his tagelmust.

The startled photographer jumped off the wall, fumbling through his pockets, then shyly approached me with a coin. I made a great show of examining it, holding it up to the light, and even biting it as I had seen in a movie long ago. Finally tucking it into the folds of my robe, I stood tall in the saddle, striking my best warrior pose, and said, "OK, take photo!" The man clicked away as the three of us rode past him, with Halis no longer able to control his laughter and even Mahmoud giggling under his breath.

That poor gentleman who thought he had just taken a National Geographic photo of a lord of the desert will never know he had just shot a middle-aged white guy from Los Angeles.

The three of us arrived at my hotel, laughing so hard that tears now streaked Halis' face. We parted ways with plans to reunite that evening for a farewell dinner, my thank you for such an amazing journey. I spent most of the afternoon thinking of a proper tip to give Halis and Mahmoud, realizing they most likely would prefer receiving a goat instead of money, when a truly original idea struck me.

I was carrying a portable hard drive full of photos of whales I had taken on a previous trip to Mexico. I doubted either of these desert nomads who lived in a landlocked country had ever seen the ocean, let alone a whale. When they arrived I plugged my hard drive into the tiny 12-inch black and white TV, and there, in a Timbuktu hotel, proceeded to show them dozens of whale photos.

These two hardened warriors, with daggers stuck in their waist bands, sat cross legged on my bed, giggling like small children at recess, yelling at each new image, pointing at the screen and poking each other with unabashed glee. They bounced up and down and I was overjoyed at their unexpected exuberance. They were particularly taken with the shots of 40-ton whales breaching, and asked how could they do this?

With nothing to compare this to they called them big fish, and when they asked how large they really were, I recalled that we had crossed the Niger river together and had seen hippopotamus. I said that the whales were many times larger, but am not sure they believed me.

They stared in open-mouthed amazement, not only at the photos of whales, but equally at the fact that I could put such pictures on an electronic screen. For these men who mixed Islam with superstition, desert myth and ancient ceremony, what I was giving them was tantamount to magic.

We were having such a great time that when we finished the local restaurants were closed, but it did not matter. We all embraced with oaths of eternal friendship and I watched as they walked off into the humid night, chattering like jaybirds until becoming silhouettes against the mud city.

I went to my bed smiling, grateful for the surreal worlds we had introduced each other to, and felt it was a great exchange.

James Michael Dorsey (jamesdorsey.com) is an award-winning author, photographer and lecturer. He has traveled extensively in 45 countries, mostly far off the beaten path. His main pursuit is visiting remote tribal cultures in Asia and Africa. He is a fellow of the Explorers Club, a former director of the Adventurers Club and a travel consultant to Brown & Hudson of London. He lives in Culver City, CA.

NAYANNA CHAKRBARTY

PILGRIMAGE TO MOUNT KAILASH
Tibet

Day 12: At this altitude, the ballpoint pen has dried up. A pink highlighter has come to my rescue. When this dries up, what if I dip the felt nib in water, will it still work?

The journey to Tibet has been a torturous one. The non-stop drive in an all-terrain vehicle has caused an injury to my left shoulder and has bruised my knee. I had believed that sitting at the window seat would be a good idea to get a glimpse of the terrain, to capture memorable photographs and to rejoice with the glorious valleys. But the extreme terrain had no mercy. Apart from the turbulent mountain roads, which has caused my head to get slammed several times to the roof of the car, I had also swayed into a fellow passenger's lap whenever the car had turned right. When it was a left turn, three passengers had slammed into me.

I thought that holding onto the handle above the door would have given me better support. However, as I had been clenching it too hard, the sudden turns had made my shoulder sore. The handle to operate the window kept hitting my knee constantly and that has caused knee soreness.

So, on day 12, I remind myself that this is just the journey, tomorrow will be the real challenge — the climb around Mount Kailash.

*****

The moon looks glorious tonight and its reflection on Manasarovar Lake is heavenly. I cannot stay out long because the extreme cold weather is already giving me a nose bleed. Taking a dip in this water is an important step in this journey. We have collectively decided the time to take the dip in the morning.

Many group members have made up their minds to stay back at Manasarovar Lake's campsite. The altitude sickness has been merciless for some. Others have lost their confidence to walk for the next three days to complete this spiritual expedition. Those who have decided to stay back prefer to take the dip at noon, since by then the sun would be up and the lake would be warmer. I find this hilarious and an impossible assumption. How can the sun heat up such a large water body in this frigid weather? But I decide to keep silent and dismiss. Five of us decide that we should wake up early, around 4 a.m., and take the holy dip.

Day 13: It is dark and cold when someone whispers close to my tent, "Wake Up."

"Yeah, OK, I'm up."

I step out, dressed in a humble T-shirt and track pants. I feel the chilled Himalayan wind punch me hard on my rib cage; I tremble. The intense pain travels to my eardrums and makes my skin burn. I reassure myself that just having taken off three layers of woolens and unzipped from the warmth of my double-layered sleeping bag, I now need time to get acclimated. Three of us approach another tent to wake up the woman from Ireland who earlier had agreed to join us.

"It is too cold, I can't do this," she whispers. "You guys go on."

It is windy and we decide not to go to the next tent to wake anyone, thus heading straight to the lake. The torch light guides us. The Londoner takes off his shoes, steps into the water and instantly pulls back. His reaction looks as if something has bitten him.

"What? Are you hurt?" I ask.

"It's freezing, let's not do this," he says.

The other man agrees.

I think to myself, "What if we don't come by this path again after the trek and the Sherpas take us back by another route? I will miss this opportunity to seek the blessing of these sacred waters. I have come too far to give up now."

"OK, boys, I will give it a try," I say.

"You will freeze. The trek is important..... Listen."

I walk straight ahead in pitch darkness and leave my slippers somewhere. But when my toes touch the water, I understand what the fuss is all about. Sheer numbness grips my reflexes. I feel nothing. Correction, panic is setting in. Before the true message of frigidness reaches my brain, paralyzing me in pain, I immerse my entire body, from head to toe, in the water. I come up and repeat this twice in complete darkness. I think of nothing, nor worry about consequences. I have to do this, that's all I know.

I walk back, drenched in the pure Himalayan waters.

"You are insane," says the other guy, while the Londoner only shakes his head.

As we zip ourselves back into our individual tents, I start feeling the chill all over my body. I quickly undress from the wet clothing and begin wearing the woolens. I get in the sleeping bag, wear three layers of socks and two woolen caps. But this miserable chill is still ruthless. My hair is still wet and that sets off an uncontrollable shiver, followed by the chattering of my teeth. I am so cold that the thermals, three layers of sweaters, a duck-feathered coat, two heavy knit scarves and gloves still can't shield the chill. I lie alone in darkness, pathetically helpless. The batteries of my defenseless torch have given up on me a long time ago. The wind blows tremendously and the tent caves into me. I feel the immense power of the Himalayan wind, which can take me adrift with my tent somewhere.

I wait for my body to settle down, which feels like eternity. I don't know what is worse, the shivering or my teeth chattering. Finally, it is dawn; I can see the color of the tent again. The Sherpas are talking in whispers and setting up the fire for breakfast.

I sip hot milk, sitting by the crackling fire, watching the oats get cooked, when someone pats my shoulder. "You survived." It is the other guy who didn't dare to venture in, seeing the Londoner yelp in the cold water. I smile.

The sensation of the hot milk traveling from my throat into the inner layers of my stomach is very soothing but this relief is short-lived. Suddenly, it begins to rain. There is no refuge. The tents have been packed and loaded in the trucks. I hurriedly gulp my milk before it gets diluted in the downpour. We stand in the rain for a while, then we decide to go ahead lest we lose daylight to reach the camp at night.

The significance of Mount Kailash is of a spiritual nature. The faithful of Hinduism, Buddhism and Jainism, including the Boras, believe this mountain to be holy and a source to gain spiritual guidance.

The four-wheel-drive struggles over the slush, spinning its wheels. Constantly dreading the fear of having to push a vehicle stuck in deep mud, our fingers crossed, we manage to reach Darchen. It stops raining and the sun comes up. The upcoming trek around Mount Kailash is 52 kilometers (30 miles). The journey is going to be spread over three days.

The snow on the mountaintop glistens under the sun, and all the hardships don't seem to matter anymore. After a final head count, the team leader discusses the options of hiring personal guides. I feel it is a good idea to have some company on this long, treacherous journey.

Prema, a woman in her early-20s, her 5-year-old son Thantri, and their mountain dog Ouna are my companions. She has a contagious smile, and her mischievous little boy adds a bit of mystery to the travel. Our conversations are limited to nods and hand gestures as she speaks in an unknown dialect. The Sherpas from Nepal don't seem to follow what she says either. My connection with her and her son is beyond the barriers of verbal language. It is a feeling of togetherness, to reach a common goal.

"At last, Mount Kailash, up close and personal," I think.

With renewed enthusiasm, I start my walk, as I enjoy the golden sunshine and rejoice the blue sky. The clouds glide smoothly, as they play hide and seek with the snow. The Himalayan winds join in the game, only to disperse the fluffy clouds away. It behaves like a bully. I feel the tranquility around is a sign of divine energy. In this serene silence, I can only hear my breathing. My pace slows down as the ground starts to get steep. I need frequent breaks to catch my breath. The air is thinning

PILGRIMAGE TO MOUNT KAILASH 263

and the intensity of the sun is heightening. I stuff all my woolens into the backpack. Prema hands me the water bottle, which I had filled in the morning. After the merciless shiver at dawn, I had decided to fill steaming hot water in the flask. Now, that decision makes me feel worse as the temperature soars.

After three hours of walking, I am exhausted. I sit on a rock resting, waving at all the fellow trekkers passing me by. Realizing that I am left behind, Prema signals me to get up.

"Five minutes more." I say, gesturing with my fingers.

She shakes her head and answers with her thumbs down. I laugh. "OK, you win."

I reach the base camp after six hours. The Sherpas had already set up the tents and had begun cooking dinner. The sun sets; my fellow travelers huddle into their sleeping bags to regain their strength for tomorrow. I sit gazing up at the bright, twinkling stars, the glorious moon and Mount Kailash. The aura of the mountain is mesmerizing. The more I gaze, the more I understand that I am a chosen one. This placidity is my definition of ultimate peace.

Day 14: The Sherpas bang on metal plates to wake us up.

"We have to start early, it is going to be a long day," yells the team leader.

I had stopped looking at my wristwatch from Day 2 of the journey. Time is of no essence when one is away from civilization. The sun rises and Mount Kailash bathes in the dawn's orange hue. The transformation of the snow from white to the glorious shades of the sun's rays is remarkable. The changes take a few minutes, but leave a lasting impression.

Today, the trek is to the Droma La Pass around 5,650 meters (3.5 miles). The climb is extremely steep, and within a few minutes of walking, I need to rest. I have to cross over a hillock to be on the main trail. I am extremely breathless, panting hard to take in air. I try to calm myself, drinking hot water from the flask. My thirst is unquenchable and I leave very little water to suffice for the rest of the day. I start again, climbing over boulders, skipping the sharp, jagged stones. However, my energy is short-lived. I stop to rest again. The whole group overtakes me; I remain in solitude.

It is really difficult. I think, "It's time to give up."

A Sherpa who usually walks in the middle of the group to make sure everyone is accounted for whistles from the top of the hillock.

"Only few steps. No rest," he yells.

I wave back. I am too breathless to complain.

"Take small steps. Don't stop."

This renews my spirit. I slowly follow the encouraging words of the Sherpa and somehow drag myself to reach the top of the hillock. Now, I realize the mammoth task of the day is to trek across the deep gorge and reach the other side of the mountain.

My body, slowly but steadily, is getting accustomed to the low oxygen levels and I finally reach Droma La Pass. The area is decorated with multicolored flags like the ones I have witnessed in many Buddhist monasteries. Prayers are chanted and the fragrance of incense delights my tired senses.

The next challenge is going down the mountain range. There is no trail to follow. It is a perilous, long way down. The end of this steep descent resembles a bottomless pit. It is nerve-racking not to know where I am going to end up. Tightly, I hold onto Prema's hand and plunge ahead. I try to imagine I am on a water slide, but the sound of the stones crunching under our body weight makes it impossible for me to get distracted and dive into my creative imagination. The larger stones loosen along, rolling down rapidly.

I slip, get up bruised and balance myself again, only to slip farther down. But the end is far from over. I tumble down, landing flat on my back again and again. The loose stones add to the momentum, but their jagged edges also act as speed-breakers. The final topple is in high speed, and I grab a shrub to slow down. Finally, I succeed in reaching the end and stand on a rugged plateau. My right palm feels an intense burning sensation. "Perhaps, I cut myself," I think. However, when I examine my palm, I discover a mesh of small, white thorns clinging to the surface of my skin.

The shrub I grabbed had a soft, velvety texture but it was deceptive. When I look closely, I discover the spiky thorns. I believe the shrubs seek revenge on those who pull and uproot them for their personal gain and I am the guilty victim of the day. The sting is excruciating; my palm swells and begins to itch.

Prema quickly points to a flowing stream. I wash my hand thoroughly, but the melting ice water makes it worse. I sit on a boulder, wrap my arms around my body and bury my head between my knees, trying hard to overcome the pain.

The sun's harsh glare further adds to my hardship. Sweat trickles through the layers of my woolens. As I start to take off my jacket, the chilly wind sweeps across my fatigued body, almost pushing me down. The melting snow makes the ground slippery and I crawl on all fours to block the high-velocity winds.

After walking endlessly for 10 hours, I manage to reach the campsite at sunset. Every inch of my body aches. My nerves writhe in pain and my mind hibernates into a blank state. The glacial wind embraces my weary body, making me tremble again, while my sore, itchy palm reminds me of my frail consciousness.

Day 15: Today, we return to base camp. Several members of the group who were unable to join this crucial journey had handed to me their family photographs, so that they could be a part of the pilgrimage in spirit.

The trail is flat and fairly easy to walk on, or is it my mind and body growing accustomed to the physical hardships of high altitude and wilderness?

I see Prema pick up small, colored stones from the path. I signal her. "What are these? Why are you collecting?" She shows me a pendant made from one of these stones around her neck. I realize and understand that everything on this route has divine blessing. I pocket a few to take back home to friends and family.

In three hours, I reach the end of the route. The vehicles are ready to take all of us back to the Manasarovar campsite. I take a moment to thank the presiding Deity for this magnificent journey.

Over the years, whenever I think of this expedition, I get truly emotional. It leaves me wondering how I was able to manage it all alone. It is only by His Grace that such a strenuous journey was possible successfully.

"If you believe…you shall find." This is the lesson I have learned from this remarkable pilgrimage to Mount Kailash.

Nayanna Chakrbarty, an international writer who lives in Mumbai, celebrates 10 years of creative writing success in 2014. She also is a closet daredevil, who springs into action when confronted with roller coasters, torrent whirlpools, Himalayan mountain terrains and deep ocean diving. Her website is original-writer.com.

MICHAEL ENGELHARD

HONEYMOON FOR THREE
Alaska, USA

Below us, a tundra mosaic unfolds in 100 hues of brown and green, mixed with the unblinking blue of melt water ponds. Frost heaves or pingos blister the land, interrupting its polygon patterns. Willow patches cling to rivers whose braids unravel with distance. Above the horizon, the peaks of northern Alaska's Brooks Range hover like long-held wishes come true.

Our pilot Bob is an old hand — a "sourdough" as they call them up here — with the frame and facial hair of a "griz." He turns to me, nods. I can see myself duplicated in his insect-eye aviator glasses, dwarfed by the immensity outside the cockpit. A toothy grin splits his furred face.

We took the regular twin-prop from Fairbanks, where I was waiting for my summer guiding schedule to fill. On its way north, the plane crossed the Yukon River and flew high above the pipeline that leads to Prudhoe Bay. Whittling away at pale, spruce-covered bluffs, the great river rolled placidly westward to its appointment with the Bering Sea. After a brief stop in Bettles, on the airfield that served as a way station for U.S. warplanes sent to Russia during World War II, we switched to Bob's single-engine Cessna with floats, chartered through an outfitter.

"So, when are you guys gonna be at the Alatna?" our pilot comes in over my headset, between bouts of static.

I shudder and roll my eyes to get my brother's attention.

"What do you mean, 'Alatna'? We were planning to hike to the John, where you are supposed to drop off our boats and supplies for the river leg of this trip."

"Right. No problem," drawls the voice in my ear.

He pulls on the horn, the plane banks into a steep easterly turn, and gravity pushes me into the seat. On the instrument panel, the artificial horizon is tilting like unbalanced scales when the stalling alarm goes off. I catch a glimpse of my brother. His eyes seem to plead. "I hope you know what you are doing," they say.

They are on their honeymoon, Andrew and Kerstin, my pert, curly-haired sister-in-law. This is to be the adventure heralding an even bigger one: a life spent together. I know the area between Gates of the Arctic National Park and the middle reaches of the Koyukuk River from my research in several native communities and agreed to be their guide — on the ground and water, but not up here. They are kin, and I hold myself responsible for their safety and well-being. Right now, I worry about the male gene pool of our family evaporating in a big ball of fire.

Before long, the plane loses altitude, diving straight for a chain of glacial lakes that separates foothills and plains from the gray granite of the Endicott Mountains. I crane my neck to scan the surrounding slopes for wildlife. Bob zeroes in on one of the glassy surfaces. When the floats touch down, spray obliterates our bird's shadow on the water. With the engine throttled, we taxi to shore.

As we unload backpacks and sort through piles of food, I notice movement from the corner of my eye. Turning toward it, I catch a stately caribou bull splashing into the shallows before throwing itself into the deep. It cuts straight across the lake, and the V of its wake twinkles in the rich afternoon light. Only the head and sweep of antlers are showing, like a hunk of branched driftwood. Not far behind, a grizzly comes crashing through the underbrush, desperate for a meal. The ease and speed of this bolt of taut muscle are breathtaking — at a short distance, it could out-gallop a horse. Without hesitation, Old Silvertip plunges in and streaks after the bull.

"I'll keep her running," Bob shouts over the engine's growling. "Just in case."

Dumbstruck and momentarily frozen in place, all three of us think that this is a good idea.

By the time Andrew has rummaged through his backpack and pulled out the camera, the bear and its intended dinner are too far away for a decent shot. When I clip the economy-size can of pepper spray to my pack, it seems awfully puny.

"Got your hot sauce," Bob jokes, "to spice up his dinner?" I think he means us.

Before we part, I point out to him the rendezvous place on the map.

"See you guys in a week, then."

"Headwaters of the John!"

"The John. Right."

We shake his calloused paw, and watch as he folds his bulk back into the cockpit.

Too soon for us to feel ready, the engine's droning ebbs and dies, and the plane shrinks to a speck in the distance. Only the smell of kerosene lingers. Silence reigns again, accentuated by the whine of mosquitoes. Worn out from two flights and spooked by our introduction to nature's way of doing business, we decide to spend the night here. While Kerstin and I set up the tents, Robert Redford assembles his rod and reel and starts casting for grayling or trout.

"You might want to put on some bug dope, or better yet, gloves and a hat," I say.

"In a minute. Just a few more."

We end up having good old Macs-n'-Cheese — without fish—inside their roomy honeymoon suite. My brother's hands are almost too swollen to hold a spoon.

His usually gaunt face looks puffy and flushed, and I bet he is running a temperature.

"Told you so, city slicker."

"Whatever."

Later, stretched out in my pup tent, I contemplate our arrival. Hard to believe that only this morning, I awoke in a bed in the city. Through my fly screen I watch a lazy sun grazing the world's edge without ever dipping below. Light dense and golden floods the enclosed space. Shadows on the ground outside mimic the lengthening summer days. The sky glows lavender, unencumbered by clouds, while famished hordes hit the tent fly, sounding like rain.

Our route to the headwaters is a treeless Via Dolorosa. Distance north of the Arctic Circle often is measured in pints of sweat and blood. We mostly hike, looking like beekeepers, dolled-up in rain gear, gaiters, gloves, head nets and hats, with temperatures approaching 90 degrees Fahrenheit. The only alternative is an insect repellent with DEET, a chemical compound the U.S. Army developed after the Pacific War. Its side effects can include hallucinations, insomnia, mood disturbances and seizures, a few of which have ended in death. It dissolves plastic zippers and leather and is probably a derivative of DDT or Agent Orange. People with Ph.D.s worked on this "Jungle Juice" — the bugs seem to like it. Indian old-timers have told me that, to keep mosquitoes away, they would carry a can of smoldering tree fungus in the bottom of their boats. But there's no tree fungus to be found here, because there are no trees.

Boots are forever soaked in this marshy terrain — squish, squish, squish . . . squelch goes the soundtrack for our hike. Only surface layers of soil thaw under the 24/7 stare of the arctic midsummer sun. Because the permafrost underneath never melts, water pools on the tundra with nowhere to drain — perfect breeding grounds for the beasts. Atop this gigantic sponge, we barely find enough level, dry ground to pitch our tents. When there are no mosquitoes, horseflies the size of June bugs plague us, or else tiny no-see-ums. The insects appear to be working in shifts. On a good day, there are common flies. Each night, before we slip into our sleeping bags, we check for mold growing between our toes.

Tussocks promise dry crossings of the soggy flats, but walking on them resembles balancing on camel humps. Stepping into the mud pockets in-between is not a good option either; it feels like post-holing in snow, and boots get soaked within minutes. Stepping dead center onto the mop heads seems the trick to avoid sprained ankles and wet feet. With each step, however, a voracious cloud lifts from a tussock. Every few hundred yards or so, I need to stop, wheezing like an asthmatic. I am also miffed that I have to take in the scenery filtered through a head net. (After Andrew developed the photos from our trip, he found most of them ruined, stippled with dots like black snow.)

We've perfected the cook-dinner-dressed-to-the-gills-and-dive-headlong-into-the-tent-without-spilling-the-beans act, and by now, it has become routine. Before we even sample the first spoonful of stews I concoct from dehydrated ingredients, we purge the tent of intruders. Bugs already sated by their meal leave crimson smears on the tent walls when we squeeze life out of them. We learn that the big, clumsy ones that survived the winter are not nearly as agile or vicious or numerous as this year's batch. In the mornings, we break camp in a hurry to get moving and escape our pursuers for a while, literally itching to go.

Make no mistake; these are not your garden-variety mosquitoes — they rank among the fiercest of North America's 150 species. Gone are the times when we joked about Alaska's vampire "state birds," or the leg hold trap-key rings to capture them that are sold in Fairbanks curio shops. The single-strike kill record on our trip stands at 34.

In a place where storytelling explains the world and alleviates long, dark nights, people remember how mosquitoes first came to be. According to one myth, an Eskimo man stabbed a cannibal monster after learning about its Achilles' heel. "Though I am dead," said the giant, "I will keep on eating you and all other humans forever." The man then cut the body into pieces, which he burned in a fire. When he tossed the resulting ashes into the wind, each flake became a mosquito.

Scratching my bites till they're raw, it helps to see "purpose" even in these pests. Without them, and without winter's dark moods, Alaska would be as crowded as Colorado or Wyoming, playgrounds for the newly rich and eternally bored. Like bears, those largest predators on the tundra, the smallest ones keep us humble. They remind us that we are still part of the food chain — and not necessarily at the top. In a beautiful democracy of predation, mosquitoes feed on grizzlies as well as on us; their pond-born larvae — myriads of wriggling question marks — in turn sustain thousands of shorebirds and their chicks.

The nearly featureless landscape that harbors mosquito eggs throughout subzero winters keeps unfurling, doing its best to deny us progress. With nothing but nondescript hills around, it is hard to identify landmarks for taking compass bearings, and the maps often are no help. We zig and then zag repeatedly, attempting to correct our course. At some point, Kerstin throws down her pack, sits on a hummock, and breaks into tears.

"Wilderness — I had no idea what you meant. No trails — anywhere. I want trees!"

I feel sorry for her. At times like these, I feel sorry for myself.

For good measure, the only non-stinging wildlife we encounter after our run-in at the lake is a solitary moose. It looks scrawny enough to act as a stand-in for the one from the opening credits of "Northern Exposure."

More than a week and who knows how many miles later, we top yet another rise of the endless expanse. Below us, Paradise: Black Spruce, scraggly as bottlebrushes — the first trees since we left Fairbanks. A lake tucked into a silvery crook of the John River. Finally! The put-in for the river leg of our journey. We may be running a day or two late; we don't know exactly. The only watch we carry does not show dates. Close to shore, we come upon two canoes with the outfitter's logo, several bear-proof barrels of food, and, I hope, a shipment from the blood bank.

After a layover day at the depot, splurging on fresh veggies and fruit, resting sore muscles and airing out feet, we take some practice turns on the lake. Neither of the honeymooners has ever been in a canoe. Afterward, we portage to the river, load up and shove off. By the time we join the main current, the bugs have let up considerably.

The honeymoon, however, is far from over.

Andrew and Kerstin share one canoe, while I paddle the other. Or try to. A few strokes out, I realize that the load is unbalanced, too far back in the boat and listing to starboard. The bow is too light, which becomes a problem when a headwind starts up. Gusts spin the canoe like a compass needle until it points upriver — due north. I curse and swear and keep turning it downstream, falling quickly behind. Upset, I paddle frantically, uncoordinated, only to capsize. I take a mouthful of John River that is half ice water, half glacial silt.

As soon as we've righted the boat and fished my sodden belongings from an eddy, we re-shuffle the seating arrangements. All three of us now ride in one canoe, with myself in the middle. Around these parts, this is known as the "missionary position." In the old days, greenhorns in black robes and clutching Bibles always rode mid-ship, while their stoic-faced Indian guides propelled the craft with deft strokes, biting their lips to keep from laughing. We hitch the second canoe to our stern with its bowline, towing it along. Here we are: three white folks coming down the river, one sopping wet, all looking like fools. But at the moment, nobody seems to be watching.

I am having a bad flashback to a solo trip on the Noatak River the year before. Rounding a bend in the river, I'd come face to face with a grizzly sow and her cub. They were swimming across the narrow channel, black noses poking from the water. The current kept sweeping me onward, swiftly and relentlessly, despite much frantic back-paddling. I was clearly set on collision course. The sow took one good look, judged our respective courses, and decided to return to the side from which they had come. Back on the cutbank she shook her massive head, shedding water like an overgrown Saint Bernard. One last glance over her shoulder, and she'd sauntered off into the bushes, her fuzzy offspring glued to her heels.

The scenario of a snarling mess of bear, rope, honeymooners and boats so far from help brings cold sweat to my brow.

Several miles downstream, we are well into the tree line. Because we are no longer used to vegetation higher than knee level, the sky appears pinched and somehow diminished. The stream roils complacently under our keels, slipping across gravel bars, wheeling around bends, weaving and murmuring, grabbing clods of dirt here and there, unhurried, but preoccupied with its destination. It leaves sandbars exposed, vibrating fallen trees as it passes. Such "strainers" can easily become death-traps, pinning or flipping canoes and pushing swimmers' heads underwater. The whack! of a beaver tail feels like a slap in the face, asking me to pay attention. The sound almost makes me drop my paddle, but the culprit remains invisible.

Days later, we pull out at the confluence of the John and the Koyukuk River. Bettles lies several miles upstream from this junction. We could line our canoes, along the Koyukuk's brushy banks, but I decide to forego the ordeal and blow a wad of cash instead.

"Let's call a taxi," I say.

"Have you been drinking?" Andrew asks, concern rumpling his face. He knows I don't own a satellite phone or even a cell phone.

Near a meat cache on stilts and a log cabin, I locate the weatherproof box I knew would be there, clamped to the trunk of a tall spruce. An antenna extends above the tree's top, and a solar panel close by fuels the contraption. Hi-tech has found its way into the bush. I open the box, lift the receiver, and almost instantly talk to our outfitter in Bettles.

"I'll be there in an hour," he says and hangs up.

"Another chatterbox," I mutter to myself.

"I wonder if you could have ordered us pizza," Kerstin chimes in.

Soon after we have finished unloading the canoes, a decked aluminum skiff rounds a bend in the river. With it, noise has returned. But we relish the moment, ready for beer, a shower and a bunk bed, in that order.

"Guess you found the boats all right," our chauffeur greets us, throwing me a line.

We strap both canoes to the skiff's cabin roof and take off. As the boreal forest zips by in a blur and the wind musses my hair, an emotion like regret washes over me. It could be a long time before I find myself up north again — if ever — as life has a tendency to intervene with even our best-laid plans. Despite the past weeks' discomforts, I feel that something profound has ended. But for the lovebirds reclining on the front deck, wrapped up in fleece jackets and conversation, this is just the beginning.

Michael Engelhard writes from Nome, Alaska. His work has appeared in Outside, Backpacker, Sierra, National Wildlife, San Francisco Chronicle and other publica-

tions. When he is not guiding wilderness trips in the Arctic, he backpacks in the Grand Canyon, where cactus spines and blowing sand are the most common nuisances.

ROBERT N. JENKINS

DREAM AT THE END OF THE WORLD
Antarctica

Exactly 22 hours after leaving Ushuaia, Argentina, which calls itself "the end of the world," the Norwegian expedition ship Fram reached the Southern Ocean, which circles Antarctica — the real end of the world.

The captain's P.A. announcement interrupted the lecture on that frozen continent's ecology, but I silently cheered. That's because for me — and for every passenger I asked — reaching Antarctica had been an impossible dream.

When we reached the Southern Ocean — the water temperature dropped an astonishing 7 degrees when we entered that continental current — Fram was little more than halfway to our first trip ashore. That meant I might be facing another night and day like the first one — grabbing for corridor handrails or the backs of chairs to brace against the exaggerated rolling of the ship in what can be the planet's most hostile 600 miles of sea.

But Fram's progress also meant I was that much closer to a continent so massive that if you put the United States on top of Antarctica, there would be more than a million-and-a-half square miles uncovered. Meanwhile, the U.S. would be sitting on ice more than a mile-and-a-half thick.

I'd be landing in early summer — when the temperature would climb to freezing only one of our four days there.

I could barely wait.

My patience was tested the next morning while the ship was still approaching: It motored into a mini-blizzard whose tiny snowflakes turned to sleet so thick the Fram seemed fogbound. The deck became slippery with snow.

I felt some apprehension: What had I gotten myself into? This continent's climate claimed human lives, and the seas that had to be crossed had already tested my resolve about experiencing a Bucket List adventure.

However, once the Fram passed the storm and reached the islands off the Peninsula, I understood what Dorothy felt as she opened the farmhouse door: I found myself under a brilliant blue sky in a majestic land, its horizons defined by mountains and perennial winter.

Huge granite peaks, whose jagged outlines were softened by thick coats of snowdrift, were all around. Icebergs glistened pearly white or an eerie neon tur-

END OF THE WORLD 285

quoise, or both. Irregular clangs and chungs sounded throughout the 373-foot-long ship as its hull plowed through drift ice, remnants of building-sized icebergs still within view.

I could see penguins leaping above the surface of the clear sea for fractions of a second before darting ahead, underwater.

My apprehension had been replaced by joy and excitement. I was enthralled.

My eight-day voyage had become an expedition. And on expeditions there are often surprises.

*****

"All stated times and activities are changeable due to weather conditions, or other circumstances out of our control," the daily agenda reminded passengers.

That's why the captain slowed the Fram on Day 3 so we could trail three fin whales. And that's why the much-awaited scenic cruise through the 7-mile-long Lemaire Channel in the eight-passenger landing boats was canceled both on the night of Day 5 and the next morning. As the 122 passengers swarmed the three observation decks to stare at a monster slab of ice a mile or so in front of the bow, the captain explained over the P.A.:

"Well, this is what happens when a 500-meter-wide iceberg enters a 550-meter-wide channel. We cannot send in the little boats because they must always be near the big ship.

"We will turn and go the long way to the other end of the Lemaire Channel. And tomorrow, we will see if the iceberg has taken a holiday somewhere else."

On expeditions, however, surprises happen.

So, the layers of gray clouds suddenly blew away to reveal another sunny day.

"If we get a third day like this, then don't ever come back here, because we will never get it this good again,'' said the assistant expedition leader, Ina Schau Johansen.

She wasn't joking. On the voyage preceding ours, those passengers had had only two hours of sunlight during their four days of landings.

But on this, our sunny third day, in place of the canceled small-boat cruise of the Lemaire Channel, everyone could get a sightseeing trip in the craft among icebergs large and small.

A favorite image: a single Gentoo penguin on a sizable flat-topped 'berg floating near the Fram. Although I had already viewed and photographed thousands of the little critters during landings, I felt the image of just a single Gentoo was special.

I had only seen them in uncountable numbers, in their rookeries. But here in front of me were two symbols of an entire continent — a penguin and an iceberg. It was moving, a counterpoint to the vastness of this land.

*****

Because Antarctica wildlife is protected against harm, we passengers were repeatedly told to keep at least 15 feet from the penguins and their "highways" — the narrow paths they created as they waddled between nest and sea.

Penguins won't nest directly on snow, lest that cold prevent their eggs from hatching. Instead, the mature birds will even climb steep hills to find bare rock on which to create their nests.

The construction materials are pebbles and small rocks the male carries, one at a time, in his beak. The guy with the coolest rock nest gets the girl. After she lays an egg, they take turns sitting on it, while the other penguin goes to the sea to feed.

Something not mentioned in those wildlife documentaries on TV is that as cute as penguins are, their rookeries, or nesting colonies, stink.

Nope, no other word for the odor.

The penguins' chief food is a creature named krill. But penguins only partially digest the krill and then poop wherever they happen to be.

During breeding and chick-rearing times, the penguins spend most of their time in the rookeries. The resulting ammonia/rotten-fish stench is another instance when Antarctica took my breath away.

But the deep snow to trudge (I often broke through the crust, going knee-deep), hills to climb and the odor are mere annoyances compared to the excitement of being near the rookeries.

Just watching the penguins waddle along from side to side, or slide on their bellies down hills, or hop over some impediment made me smile.

*****

Originally, I didn't think our time ashore would be so rewarding. On the first landing, the 32-mph wind dropped the wind-chill to 60 degrees Fahrenheit below freezing. Dense clouds at first hid the sun.

On the days when the weather and landscape were most challenging, or when we plowed through 30-foot waves, I would feel embarrassed to step into either of the Fram's elevators.

In each was a 5-foot-tall headshot of one or the other of Norway's most famed polar explorers, Roald Amundsen and Fridtjof Nansen. Each had sailed on wooden ships named the Fram — Norwegian for "forward."

In the photographs, each man looked out with weather-worn faces and hard eyes. I felt they were challenging me for daring to come to Antarctica in so much comfort.

Those men, and other European and American explorers of more than a century earlier, came in too-fragile sailing ships, wearing animal skins over woolen clothes, without my ship's redundant engines and satellite links, without at least three hot entrees at every meal, without hot showers.

Those explorers were more than just courageous and hearty souls — they were risking their lives. And many of them lost that gamble.

So, finally, I felt privileged to have barely sampled what they had chosen to endure for months on Antarctica. Its magnificence does that to you.

Robert N. Jenkins lives in St. Petersburg, Fla. In a 39-year career at the St. Petersburg Times, he served as editor of national news, state news, features and, for 19 years, travel editor. His section and his own writing won eight Lowell Thomas travel journalism awards. He has cruised on about 70 ships to write about them, has walked among polar bears in Canada and on the rooftops of Stockholm's Old Town. He has no Bucket List. His four e-books are illustrated anthologies of earlier articles. They are available at Amazon Kindle, Barnes & Noble Nook and Smashwords sites.

DAVID RICHARD TEECE

FAREWELL TOUR
Turkey

I've been driving for about an hour from the Kayseri airport straight into the heart of central Turkey's Cappadocia region when the scenery shifts from standard-issue, rolling-hill farmland into something straight out of Middle Earth. High cliffs and bizarre rock spires (known as "fairy chimneys") suddenly spring up around me in a landscape that looks like it was co-designed on a dare by Salvador Dali, Frank Herbert and Dr. Seuss — after they dropped acid and followed up with a three-day drunk.

"Wow!" I say out loud, like a 5-year-old let loose at Disney World. As there is no one in the car to hear me, I seem compelled to keep saying it again and again. Wow.

I stop the car on the side of the road. "Look!" I say out loud to no one, pointing up the side of a cliff. "A cave!"

Look, a cave? I sound like one of the Hardy Boys.

I will shortly learn that saying "Look! A cave!" in Cappadocia is the functional equivalent of driving into Iowa and saying "Look! Corn!" There are literally thousands of caves. Tens of thousands. Carved into cliffs and rocks and underground caverns and lived in for centuries. People still live in them. Nearly every hotel room in Göreme where I'm headed is carved out of rock, including my own.

But I have been in Cappadocia for less than an hour, and right now I know none of this. I have located a cave. And I'll be damned if I'm passing up a chance to climb inside of it.

It's still winter and tourists are scarce; no other cars are in sight. A cold misty rain is falling and the ground is slick. I'm not dressed for hiking or rock climbing. But I leave my car on the side of the road, hiking across the field and climbing over the rocks.

The rocks at this particular site are cone-shaped, like the hoods of Grand Wizards at a Ku Klux Klan meeting. As I weave my way between the bizarre formations toward the cave, I would not be surprised by an appearance by the "Star Wars'" Sand People.

At first the cave looks impossible to reach, carved high into the cliff. But I spot a side entrance, accessible by a vertical climb that only looks quasi-dangerous. Yes, the shoes are all wrong; yes, the rocks are wet; yes, there is a quite a bit of scraping and sliding. But I make it up the side of the cliff, crawl through a short tunnel and emerge into an area that looks like it once was somebody's living room.

A flat rock sits in front the of the mouth of the cave overlooking the valley below, like a giant bean bag chair in front of the biggest of big-screen TVs. An opening in the ceiling of the cave leads to another level, with more tunnels between more rooms, like Habitrails for your pet hamster.

Someone at some point in the past 2,000 or so years has carved a symbol on the wall of the main room. It could be some long-forgotten religious designation; it could be the Tree of Life. For all I know it's the family crest of the Flintstones.

I take a picture of it anyway, because I find it amazing that such a thing exists. This won't be the last time that happens.

*****

I have lived in Turkey for nearly 1½ years now, but it's time to go. My residence permit is nearly expired, and I have an unquenchable desire for certain things that Turkey can't give me — namely edible Mexican food and affordable Irish whiskey.

As I'm leaving in less than two weeks, this trip to Cappadocia will serve as my Turkish farewell tour: one last chance to see the countryside, drink rakı, smoke nargile and mangle the language before heading home.

I'm planning to make the most of it.

Day One, Cappadocia Farewell Tour. The list of things I will wake up for at 4:30 in the morning is a short one. The only ones I can think of involve my bed being on fire.

But if you want to go ballooning in Cappadocia, there is exactly one time slot available: sometime before dawn. I'm told this has to do with the lack of wind, but I'm not buying it. I think the Turks just secretly enjoy torturing tourists by getting them out of bed before the chickens wake up.

They arrive at my hotel at 5 a.m. to take me to the balloon ride. Given the ridiculous hour, the high cost of the ticket and the fact that I'm being shoved into a van, I feel a little like the target of a kidnapping. Fortunately there doesn't appear to be any duct tape involved.

Not yet anyway.

The van drops me and a small group of sleepy, disoriented tourists at the offices of Voyager Balloons, joining what looks like a few hundred other sleepy, disoriented tourists. From what I can tell, other than me the only tourists willing to be rousted out of bed for a pre-dawn balloon ride are some Japanese women and a few of their compliant husbands.

Voyager Balloons is serving breakfast, which consists of hard rolls, a little cheese and a few slices of unidentifiable, pink-colored meat. I opt for a cup of tea.

I notice one of the Japanese women has brought her own supply of ramen noodles, apparently in case of just this kind of food emergency. She distributes the Cup o'

Noodles to her friends, who receive the gift like manna from heaven.

After about a half-hour we are herded back into the vans to be shuttled to the balloon launch site. It's light enough now that as we drive up we can see the balloons, lying on their sides like partially inflated beached whales. Baskets about the size of a Volkswagen bus are tied to each one.

We are directed to our designated bus baskets and beached whale balloons. Each basket is divided into four compartments (plus room for a pilot, I'm relieved to see), and each compartment holds up to five people. My assigned basket compartment-mates are a young Japanese couple, now assigned by his company to live in India; and Adam and Dana from Orlando, FL — perhaps the only other non-Japanese participants on the balloon tour.

"So, India," I say to my Japanese basket mate, Yoshi, to make conversation as we wait for the balloon to inflate. "That must be interesting."

"No!" He's shaking his head, almost violently. "India is a terrible place. The electricity goes off in the middle of the day. The food is too spicy." His wife, who seems to understand little else, nods emphatically at the India bashing.

"We leave India every chance we get," Yoshi continues as we climb into the basket. "This is why we are now in Turkey."

I think of telling Yoshi of the times the electricity in my Istanbul apartment has gone off in the middle of the day, but think better of it. The food is not particularly spicy in Turkey, so I guess they're still taking a step up.

The balloon pilot is explaining our "landing position" instructions to Adam, Dana, me and the 17 Japanese people in the basket. The instructions are in English. I'm wondering if "crouch down and grab the rope handles" possibly can't be translated.

The sun now is up and we stand waiting in our giant basket. Suddenly and without further instructions, I find myself floating in the air.

*****

Maybe one of the biggest surprises living as an expat in Turkey was how ordinary and unoriginal this decision turned out to be. There are literally 10s of thousands of (mostly European) foreigners living in the country, and you run into them everywhere: Germans, Russians, Italians, Brits, and more Americans than you might think.

For the most part, I and the rest of the *yabancı* do our best to blend in. But there are notable examples to the contrary.

The previous fall a German acquaintance was nice enough to offer to let me stay at her currently empty apartment for a week in the resort town of Didim in southwest Turkey. She had bought the apartment as "an investment," she told me; 11 months out of the year she was elsewhere and the place sat empty.

It sounded too good to be true when I looked on a map and saw that the town was on the Aegean Coast. I set off in a bus to Didim, with thoughts of, hey, maybe I'll move there.

It was too good to be true. Didim turned out to my least-favorite place in all of Turkey. Perhaps the entire world.

Imagine Corpus Christi, TX, but not even a nice part of Corpus Christi. Like North Beach without a beach. Or an ocean.

The sea, in fact, is miles away. Didim itself is inland, consisting of long, flat, treeless, shadeless, desolate stretches of land and an endless number of cookie-cutter, concrete apartment/condo developments. Many developments sit half-finished, investors apparently taking their money and moving it somewhere less depressing. Abandoned complexes are spread throughout town, separated by empty, weed-filled lots.

The actual Turks in this city seem to be in hiding, replaced by a population of loud, pasty, overweight, non-Turkish-speaking, middle-class Brits, who apparently are so desperate for sunshine that they will soak it up wherever they can, no matter how god-forsaken the surroundings.

The restaurant choices near the flat consist of two British pubs and an "Italian" pizza parlor. I check out the pubs. Every customer is a Brit well past their 55th birthday. Most appear to be drunk; all appear to have eaten their share of shepherd's pies. Rod Stewart's "Greatest

Hits" plays from a speaker over the bar in a continuous loop.

This doesn't feel like I am in Turkey. It feels like I am trapped in somewhere between "The Benny Hill Show" and one of Dante's Seven Circles of Hell.

Back in Cappadocia the expats are not nearly as conspicuous, but I still have no trouble stumbling right over them. In the little town of Göreme I walk down the hill from my cave hotel straight toward an establishment called "Fat Boys," politically incorrect down to its fat boy logo, which appears to be a whitewashed version of Fat Albert from the Cosby Kids.

Inside, a group of men around a pool table banter in English. One is large enough that I incorrectly assume he must be the bar's namesake. In two of the four corners of the room there are couches and chairs grouped together like the faux living rooms of a furniture store.

On the wall I see the flags of Tibet, Brazil, Australia and — inexplicably — Minnesota. Two women sit at a table in the middle of the bar, loudly lamenting the price of gasoline with cockney accents straight out of "My Fair Lady."

I wasn't looking for the expats, but it looks like I found them anyway.

I'm greeted in English by a man whom I spot immediately as a local. He seems pleasantly surprised when I answer and place my order in Turkish. I later learn that this is Yılmaz Şişman, the owner of the bar along with his Australian wife, Angela. Yılmaz's name, roughly translated into English, means "Indomitable Fat."

And that's how you legitimately get to own a bar in Göreme, Turkey, called Fat Boy's.

The billiard tournament continues and Eliza Doolittle and her friend are still yammering on about gas prices. But Yılmaz is friendly and lets me practice my Turkish without shame. The beer is cold, and the soccer match will be starting soon on the big-screen TV.

I decide I can live with a little English yammering in the background. I fluff up the cushions of my couch and — in Turkish, of course — order another Efes Dark from Mr. Indomitable Fat.

*****

Day Five, Cappadocia Farewell Tour. Winter has returned and the day is gray, snowy and cold. I decide this is as good a time as any to check out some of Cappadocia's 36 famed underground cities. If nothing else, I reason, the Underground People knew how to get out of the wind.

I drive to the town of Kaymaklı (inexplicably translated into English as "creamy"), where, unfortunately, the Japanese tour buses have arrived before me. Apparently it is spring break in Japan, and the underground city is filled with gaggles of young Asian women, giggling and making peace signs as they endlessly pose for pictures next to every possible underground archway.

It's like a clothed, alcohol-free, Japanese version of Girls Gone Wild.

After my second underground city in Derinkuyu I've decided that I pretty much get the idea: people lived underground and crawled through a lot of tunnels. My back hurts from bending and stooping.

I'm cold, tired and hungry, and — call me what you will — what I really want is a big steaming bowl of cafe latte. But seeing as the nearest Starbucks is several hundred miles away, I leave the underground city and wander into a nearby business that seems to be a combination tea house/souvenir stand.

Inside I see only two older Turkish men, and a woman whose head is covered with a scarf. Not a tourist is in sight. But there is a fire in the pot-belly stove in the middle of the room, and right now "warm and dry" looks pretty good to me. I take off my coat and order a tea.

The men resume speaking in Turkish after taking a moment to look me over. One resumes his apparently ongoing complaint about the general dearth of tourists other than the buses full of Japanese who apparently don't frequent his tea house. I interject from the neighboring table, in Turkish, that maybe it's still a little too cold. They both look up at me in surprise, as if by some miracle the child long believed to be deaf and dumb has finally spoken.

"You speak Turkish?" one of the men asks me. "Where are you from?"

I see he is a religious man, wearing a skull cap and fingering a string of prayer beads.

"I'm American, but I've been living in Istanbul," I tell him.

"Your Turkish is very good," he says to me. I know he's just being polite but I thank him anyway. It's not nearly as good as he thinks it is as he begins pontificating in Turkish, assuming that I understand what he's saying. I'm catching maybe 40 percent of it. Maybe.

He seems happy to have someone different to talk to; maybe his wife and friend have heard his monologues many times before. He's telling me about the weather and the history of the underground cities and all the different people who have lived throughout the centuries in what is now Turkey: Hittites, Romans, Jews, early Christians, modern Muslims.

I'm getting a little worried when his monologue turns to religion. He is still fingering the prayer beads, and the vocabulary is moving out of my range of ability. But he has a point he wants to make.

There are four great books, he tells me: the Torah, the Bible, the Koran, and one other I either can't understand or never heard of. But all of these books, he tells me, come from the same place.

Do I know Adem and Havva? he asks me. I look at him confused, thinking maybe these are friends of his from Istanbul I might have come across. I shake my head. Adem and Havva, he repeats. From the Bible. The light bulb goes off. Adem and Havva. Adam and Eve. Got it.

Adem and Havva are the parents of us all, he tells me. Arab, Turk, American, Muslim, Christian, Jew. This is why I don't understand these wars, he says. We are all the same family. Why are we killing each other? Why are we killing our own family?

I smile because I understand. But I don't know the answer to his question, and I tell him so.

He looks at my empty tea glass and asks if I would like another — this one is on him. A glass of tea costs about the equivalent of 55 cents. I thank him and accept the offer, happy that I wandered off the path in this unexpected direction.

*****

When I was back in the States the previous December, my friend Mark bought me a knife for Christmas. To fully appreciate how absurd this is, you'd have to know me, and my friend Mark. I'm not sure what a "Knife Guy" looks like, but I'm reasonably sure he doesn't look like either one of us. Outside of the kitchen cutlery drawer, I'm not sure I ever owned one.

The gift knife was way beyond the wimpy Swiss Army variety. With a wooden handle and a 4-inch flip blade, this looked more like something I'd take with me to a rumble under the Interstate. I had to look at the address on the label twice after opening the package to make sure it wasn't some kind of UPS shipping mistake.

"I have one just like it," Mark later told me, explaining the gift. "I take it hiking, and use it to cut up apples."

See, if I'm out on a hike and I want to eat an apple, I'm probably just going to bite it with my teeth, but OK. Thanks, Mark, I said, and Merry Christmas. I threw the knife in my checked luggage and headed back to Turkey.

Upon returning to Istanbul from Cappadocia to pack up my life, I have the bright idea to put all the heavy things in one carry-on bag. This way, I tell myself, they won't charge me for exceeding the checked baggage weight limit.

I am so, so, so smart. I mindlessly empty the "heavy things" from my office and desk drawer into the carry-on luggage.

The morning of my departure I'm feeling pretty good about myself for getting to the Istanbul airport with three heavy bags, checking into British Airways while incurring only a $60 bag charge, and easily clearing passport control. The good feeling, unfortunately, lasts only until my carry-on bag goes through the X-ray at the security checkpoint.

"Sir," the security agent says, stopping me. "Is this your bag?"

Before I originally left for Turkey, multiple smart-ass friends with even less knowledge about the country than I gave me some version of the following: "Turkey? How could you go to Turkey? Didn't you ever see Midnight Express?"

How ridiculous, I would reply. You're judging an entire country based on a 30-year-old prison movie? It would be like saying "How could you go to America; didn't you ever see 'Silence of the Lambs' or Beach Blanket Bingo?"

Besides, I proclaimed confidently in my very first travel blog entry: "I have promised all concerned to avoid the issue entirely by not having heroin strapped to my body as I arrive at customs."

Good plan. It's a shame I didn't say the same thing about knives.

"You have a knife in your bag?" the security officer asks me.

"A knife? I answer, in the same tone I would if she had asked me if I had a marmot in my pants. "No! No, of course I don't have a ..."

She unzips the bag and paws through the desk detritus before pulling out Mark's Christmas gift, holding it out in front of me just in case I wanted to deny it again.

"Oh. That knife."

OK quick, I say to myself: try not to look like a terrorist, try not to look like a terrorist, and try not to look like a terrorist. Dammit! Why did I grow this beard?

She unfolds the 4-inch blade from the wooden handle and brandishes it toward me. It's pretty clear that Mark's apple slicer is several steps beyond the prohibited box cutter.

"Sir," she says to me, "this is a problem."

This has turned out well, I think to myself. I joke in my first blog entry about "Midnight Express," and I'll get to write the last one from inside an actual Turkish prison. Now there's some irony for you.

"I'm sorry," I say to the officer. "I thought that was in my checked luggage. I had no idea ..." I wonder if I'm going to be forced to try to explain the Christmas gift/apple slicer story in Turkish. "Really really really sorry."

She continues to hold the knife out in front of me, now grasping it between two fingers like evidence in a murder trial. I wait for her to tell me to follow her to the interrogation/beating room, and hold my breath.

"We're going to have to take this," she says finally.

I exhale. Yes, please, take it! I'm sure I can find another way to eat apples in the wilderness without violating international criminal statutes.

"Thank you," I say as I pack up my crap and slink off toward my gate. I say it more than once, I'm sure.

I take this as a sign that it really is time to go home.

Hadı görüşürüz, everyone. See you again soon.

David Richard Teece is a former lawyer, journalist and stand-up comedian. For eight years he wrote and edited non-fiction for the Pittsburgh Press, Florida Times-Union and Corpus Christi (TX) Caller-Times. He received several writing awards as a journalist. Teece's experiences have taken him around the world. Most recently he spent two years in Turkey, completing his first novel, "Frogs in the Toaster (and Other Turkish Love Songs)." He is on the road again – this time to Spain – and working on his second novel, tentatively titled "America's Guest."

CREDITS

"Safari on Ice" by Peter Mandel, published with permission of the author. Copyright © 2009 by Peter Mandel

"Deserted in the Gobi" by Richard McCulloch, published with permission of the author. Copyright © 2014 by Richard McCulloch

"In Ruins" by Claire Ibarra, published with permission of the author. Copyright © 2014 by Claire Ibarra

"The Naked Truth" by Bruce Northam, published with permission of the author. Copyright © 2014 by Bruce Northam

"Filling in the Holes" by Janna Graber, published with permission of the author. Copyright © 2014 by Janna Graber

"Monkey Wrench" by Asia Nichols, published with permission of the author. Copyright © 2013 by Asia Nichols

"Letters from the Countryside" by Todd Pitock, published with permission of the author. Copyright © 2013 by Todd Pitock

"Hiking the Ancient Nakasendo Way" by Peter Mandel, published with permission of the author. Copyright © 2013 by Peter Mandel

"Feeling Tanzania" by Kimberley Lovato, published with permission of the author. Copyright © 2014 by Kimberly Lovato

"Stepping Up to the Challenge" by Mim Swartz, published with permission of the author. Copyright © 2014 by Mim Swartz

"Girding the Globe" by Dan Leeth, published with permission of the author. Copyright © 2000 by Dan Leeth

"Paradise Lost" by Gina Kremer, published with permission of the author. Copyright © 2014 by Gina Kremer

"Lionfish Quest" by Darrin DuFord, published with permission of the author. Copyright © 2014 by Darrin DuFord

"Healing Heights of Machu Picchu" by Erin Byrne, published with permission of the author. Copyright © 2012 by Erin Byrne

"Fear in Srinagar" by Mariusz Stankiewicz, published with permission of the author. Copyright © 2013 by Mariusz Stankiewicz

"Walks on the Wild Side" by Peter Mandel, published with permission of the author. Copyright © 2012 by Peter Mandel

"Last Trip to Venice" by Mim Swartz, published with permission of the author. Copyright © 2013 by Mim Swartz

"The Day the Earth Moved" by Aaron Paulson, published with permission of the author. Copyright © 2011 by Aaron Paulson

"Sailing Down Under" by Maggie Cooper, published with permission of the author. Copyright © 2014 by Maggie Cooper

"Of Nomads and Whales" by James Michael Dorsey, published with permission of the author. Copyright © 2013 by James Michael Dorsey

"Pilgrimage to Mount Kailash" by Nayanna Chakrbarty, published with permission of the author. Copyright © 2014 by Nayanna Chakrbarty

"Honeymoon for Three" by Michael Engelhard, published with permission of the author. Copyright © 2012 by Michael Engelhard

"Dream at the End of the World" by Robert N. Jenkins, published with permission of the author. Copyright © 2014 by Robert N. Jenkins

"Farewell Tour" by David Richard Teece, published with permission of the author. Copyright © 2013 by David Richard Teece

Other World Traveler Tales Books:

Chance Encounters: Travel Tales from Around the World (World Traveler Press, 2014)

ACKNOWLEDGMENTS

Thanks to former Denver Post Travel Editor Mim Swartz for your editing expertise and advice.

A heartfelt thanks to Ben, the man who holds my heart. Traveling with you is one of my favorite things in life. Where shall we go next? And to my three children, who are now creating travel adventures of their own. Your love and support are precious gifts.

Finally, a special thanks to my parents, who encouraged their 19-year-old to follow her dream of studying in Europe – and fostered a lifelong love of world travel.

www.ingramcontent.com/pod-product-compliance
Lightning Source LLC
Chambersburg PA
CBHW031408290426
44110CB00011B/308